Storehouses of Snow

Dr. Munn's
Expedition to Antarctica

Daniel V. Runyon

Library of Congress Cataloging-in-Publication Data

Runyon, Daniel V.
    Storehouses of Snow
ISBN: 978-1-878559-12-8

Cover and text design by Megan Filipowski
Photos by Dan Runyon
Photos prepared for publication by Kimmee Poole

Printed in the United States of America

Price: $15.00

Acknowledgements

Thanks to Dr. Munn for inviting me along on his expedition to Antarctica. Silverseas provided a safe and informative tour through some of the most dangerous places in the world.

Copy editing students at Spring Arbor University carefully worked over earlier drafts of this manuscript: Emilee Barnes, Abbey Barney, Megan Filipowski, Abbie Lynn Godmair, Victoria Miller, Kimmee Poole, Ethan Ross, Haley Taylor, and Sydney Williams. Thanks also to Renée Runyon for final proofreading.

Ultimate gratitude to the One who created and sustains the Antarctic refrigeration unit on this fine planet.

Daniel V. Runyon, 15 June 2012

Contents

Dr. Munn leaving Ushuaia

Chapter One
The Traveler

At age 83, Dr. E. Harold Munn, Jr. has done a great many things, but he has never been to Antarctica, so he books passage on the Prince Albert II out of Ushuaia, Argentina, sailing December 12, 2011.

An expedition cruise ship refurbished in 2008, the Prince Albert II is designed for navigating waters in remote destinations including polar regions. The 6,072-ton vessel has a strengthened hull with a Lloyds Register ice-class notation (1A) for passenger ships. With eight Zodiac boats for making landfall, she presents a realistic means of achieving Dr. Munn's lifelong-dream of setting foot on the fifth-largest continent. Yes, lifelong, for his father, Dr. E. Harold Munn, Sr., triggered his curiosity as a youngster by showing him film footage of Admiral Richard E. Byrd's Antarctic exploration and life at "Little America."

Getting to the Prince Albert II from Michigan requires a flight from Grand Rapids, Michigan, to Dallas, Texas, to Buenos Aires, Argentina, to Ushuaia, the southern-most city in the world in the Tierra del Fuego region of the South American continent.

Arriving at the Grand Rapids airport two hours before his December 10 scheduled flight time, Dr. Munn learns that his flight to Dallas has just been cancelled. Cancelled! Just like that. So he calmly inquires as to what measures American Airlines will take to get him to Buenos Aires in time for his early Monday morning, December 12, chartered flight to Ushuaia.

Nancy, the counter agent, starts pecking away at her keyboard and within ten minutes has him on a commuter jet to Chicago, where he can catch a flight to Miami, Florida, and thence to the capital of Argentina, arriving at 10:15 a.m. on Sunday, December 11, just 50 minutes later than originally scheduled. A couple phone calls later, he has revised arrangements for meeting his driver at the airport in Buenos Aires, negotiated his way through the extensive security measures at the airport, and trundled onto the America Eagle commuter jet to Chicago.

Excellent visibility makes the flight across Lake Michigan spectacular, the sun glistening on the slightly-rippled water. A few tiny popcorn clouds drift below the plane. The crisp, icy air and bracing winds, he knows, will soon give way to sweltering tropical heat and humidity in both Miami and Buenos Aires.

Elaborate Christmas decorations fill terminal H at O'Hare Airport in Chicago, surrounding a giant globe hanging from the ceiling and showing six detailed continents. Unfortunately, where Antarctica should have been, a small steel disk supports the sculpture—apparently the fifth-largest continent does not exist in the mind of this metal artist!

Holiday travelers scramble about in the usual fashion, and Dr. Munn makes a couple more phone calls to square things away, confirms his frequent flyer details with the gentleman at gate H11B, and settles in for the three-hour hop to Miami. Two hours into the flight, a loud noise accompanied by the cabin lights going out causes Dr. Munn to glance out his window over the wing where he detects evidence of the disintegration of the left generator: engine lubricating oil is seeping up through joints in the wing! Shortly thereafter the pilot announces the loss of a generator but that passengers should not worry, he'll have it on auxiliary power in no time. True to his word, the lights come on five minutes later.

In Miami, Dr. Munn has a sandwich and then makes his way to gate D21 to await his 11:25 p.m. disembarkation to Buenos Aires. There he learns the flight is delayed until 7:00 a.m., and that he should go to the re-booking desk near gate D14 to get his hotel voucher for the night and to make sure he will be on the morning flight.

This new flight, assuming it gets him into Buenos Aires at 5:55 p.m. as planned, will still give Dr. Munn time to get to his hotel, have some supper, and a short night of sleep before his 6:00 a.m. check-in time at the domestic airport for his charter flight to Ushuaia.

The line at the re-booking kiosk is perhaps a quarter-mile long, so as the clock steadily approaches midnight, he pulls out his camera to get a shot of the throng of mostly Spanish-speaking people who just want to go home. "I imagine these airline personnel have to deal with some pretty irate passengers," he observes as the line inches toward the counter. The airline gives him transport to the

Miami Hilton downtown, and by about 1:00 a.m. he has stood in another line to get room 103, taken a quick shower, and is fast asleep for a comfortable three-hour night. At 4:30 a.m. he is back out in front of the hotel for the 15-minute shuttle back to the airport.

Downtown Miami was dark when he arrived and is still dark as he leaves, so there's not much to observe about the city except that traffic at 4:45 a.m. on Sunday morning is very manageable. He goes through airport security, spends his breakfast voucher on scrambled eggs, toast, sausage, and orange juice, and has time for a brief nap before the flight to Buenos Aires boards about 45-minutes late.

Seat 24A is a bit cramped for a gentleman of Dr. Munn's stature, but he methodically stows his jacket, camera bag, small backpack, and travel kit containing his passport and documentation, squeezes into his narrow space, and settles in for the 11-hour flight.

Teens and adults, men and women, middle-aged and children are frustrated and challenged by the array of difficulties these travel inconveniences cause, but Dr. Munn trudges through every shifting expectation with the equanimity that has characterized his life since that day on September 7, 1928, when he was born. Having flown his own plane throughout his career as a radio broadcast consulting engineer, the world of high-tech travel holds no surprises but plenty of amusing complications.

"I apologize for the delay in boarding," says the pilot when the flight is underway. "New customs regulations require that the plane be entirely stocked for service and secured before passengers are permitted to board. The regulation was introduced last week, and the result is chaos. But now I hope you will sit back and enjoy your flight."

The flight takes him over Cuba, the Caribbean Sea, corners of Venezuela and Colombia, and over the Amazon rain forest between Iquitos, Peru, and Manaus, Brazil, a vast, vast world of green and snaking rivers. Threading its way down the eastern slopes of the Andes Mountains, the plane flies over La Paz, Bolivia, and half the length of Chile before turning east over the cities of Cordoba, Rosario, and finally to Buenos Aires, Argentina, where hundreds of miles of thriving farms and ranches spread across the land outside this city.

The customs officials will not accept his American $100 bill as partial payment for his $140, 10-year visa, so Dr. Munn pays with his credit card, and upon leaving the secure area discovers that the scheduled driver is not there to pick him up. However, a Silverseas representative from his ship is waiting to pick up another group, so he chats briefly with this gentleman, who makes a cell phone call, visits for a moment with a young clerk who seems to have expertise in these matters, and assures Dr. Munn that a ride will be available for him shortly to take him downtown to the Hotel Republica. Upon arrival at this historic location under the massive obelisk in the heart of Buenos Aires, he finds it is raining, so instead of walking in the historic city center, he orders dinner, connects to the Internet to catch up on personal and business matters, and calls it a day.

The morning wake-up call is scheduled for 5:00 a.m. for a short trip to the regional airport and the last flight that will take him to Ushuaia and the beginning of his adventures.

Argentina's dramatic coast

Chapter Two: Ushuaia
Land at the End of the World

Promptly at 5:45 a.m. the expected transport arrives,
Dr. Munn hoists himself into the van, and in due course
arrives at the Jorge Newbery Domestic Airport where he
checks his bag, has a breakfast of orange juice so thick it
requires chewing, a fruit cocktail, and a dish of yogurt. The
flight to Ushuaia is uneventful, and he is met at the air
terminal by a bus that takes him to a restaurant in the
mountains for a lunch featuring potato salad, grilled lamb,
and chocolate ice cream. Yellow buttercups blanket the
hillside, and forsythia in full bloom graces a few lawns of
wooden houses with steep metal roofs that look to have
been transplanted from Germany or Switzerland.

Following dinner he is transported to the Prince Albert
II which has been relabeled the Silver Explorer, where he
finds stateroom 407 and settles in to comfortable
accommodations with an old world feel: natural wood
paneling, a tiled bath, and rich, black-out curtains for the
coming world where there is no darkness at night. The red
parka provided by Silversea fits perfectly, the aluminum
water bottle for shore expeditions has a handy clip for

fastening to a belt loop, and the binoculars feature 10 x 50 magnification with a seven-degree field of vision.

A very thorough safety training session explains such things as the importance of not "holding" a door by the edge lest it slam in high seas and severely injure fingers, how to put on the life vest and get to a lifeboat, practical instructions on how to report an emergency, and a gentle suggestion to not mess with the sprinkler heads in the stateroom which are easily capable of filling the room with water before a message can be delivered to the bridge to shut off that particular sprinkler.

Safety is highly stressed as the ship will enter some of the most dangerous waters on the planet. Doors can withstand smoke and fire for an hour, portions of the ship can be sealed off in the event of flooding, and the two lifeboats can handle 150 people each; with 120 crew and 130 passengers, that leaves 50 or so empty seats.

Not a typical pleasure cruise, this is an *expedition*, and pains are taken to impress upon the passengers the high caliber of resources provided. The crew is truly international. The restaurant is run by a Hungarian, the supplies guy and the piano player are from the Philippines, the executive chef is from Germany, the head butler is from India, and the ship features three concessionaires: the store is run by a Brazilian, the hair dresser hails from South Africa, and the massage therapist comes by way of Ireland.

The expedition staff includes 11 people with various specializations. Yada, from north Holland, is the assistant expedition director who writes the daily *Chronicle* and handles paperwork. She pilots one of the eight Zodiacs—rubber crafts that transport explorers to shore or to get closer to whales—as do the other expedition staff. Nicki is the staff assistant from Bavaria, Germany. Ollie, from the Black Forest in the south of Germany, is a marine biologist who leads scientific diving expeditions. Canadian Shushanna Jacobs is a marine biologist specializing in eco-biology, which means she studies how animals adapt to their environment. Franz is a Bavarian German now living on the North Sea coast and is a research director in marine ornithology. "What Franz doesn't know about bird migration hasn't been discovered," expedition team leader Robin West suggests mildly.

Liz Bradfield, from Cape Cod in the United States, calls herself an "aspiring generalist" who has also published a couple books of poetry on nature and animals. Peter Damish is an American historian writing a book on polar exploration who's been fascinated by Antarctica for 40 years. His passion is history of the emotions, motivations, and things that inspire people to do what they do. He wonders aloud why anyone would take a holiday where he will freeze off his backside, and then answers himself with the claim that Antarctica is "the 10th planet" with an inexhaustible supply of wonder and beauty.

A New Zealand film photographer will document the voyage in video and photos. He calls himself a non-intrusive nature photographer. Cara Weller, of Fairbanks, Alaska, is a biologist studying whales and seals who has been coming here for 18 years. Lucki is from Argentina and now uses southern Paraguay as a base from which he does glacier research. All these folks will present lectures and lead shore excursions throughout the trip.

Excursion director Robin West, from Port Elizabeth, South Africa, ends the meeting by announcing that the lecture program starts tomorrow at 10:00 a.m.: "Read in the ship newspaper, the *Chronicle,* to find out what's going on with the lectures. You can also watch it on your interactive TV (channel 9). Tomorrow, we have the ornithologist at 10 a.m., the historian at 11:30 a.m., and the photographer at 5:00 p.m."

Briefing is every night at 6:45 p.m. and consists of a recap of the day and a summary of the next day's plans. Bad weather can delay or alter the anticipated destination, so be flexible. The expedition team is anxious to be on shore as much as possible because they are doing their own research as well as explaining things to passengers.

Robin West gives these urgent instructions: "On every expedition please always take your parka, water flask, binoculars, and backpack. Take your binoculars everywhere—even to dinner. We sometimes sight whales while we're dining. Now, about the weather: We are expecting seven to eight meter swells (30 feet) when we exit the Beagle Channel about 3:00 a.m., and when we hit the open ocean, winds of about 40 knots are expected. Secure all loose items in your suite or put them on the floor. There will be a lot of movement sideways, and while the stabilizers do help, expect a rocking boat. Once we get down to the peninsula, the weather will be better, but the first 600 miles will be rough."

West concludes his talk with this promise, delivered in his leisurely South African brogue: "You do know, of course, that once you have been on this trip, every other holiday you will ever take has been ruined! You are going to the most spectacular destination in the world. Getting there is rough, but once you arrive, expect a dramatic, gorgeous, and incredible experience. Thank you all and good night."

Dinner is served at 8:00 p.m., and on his menu for the evening Dr. Munn finds appetizers of iced beetroot soup with smoked salmon, Duck Rilette marinated with Cabernet Sauvignon jam, or sole, tilapia, and shrimp casserole with chardonnay cream, leek and carrot vermicelli; Intermezzo options include essence of Dover sole, a salad of marinated artichokes, roasted peppers, cherry tomatoes, olives, pickled onions, and chili peppers with balsamic dressing, or Cannelloni al Forno made of Ricotta Cheese and spinach with stuffed pipe noodles with Bechamel sauce, mozzarella and tomato gratin.

Following the Intermezzo, Dr. Munn is invited to cleanse his pallet with a citrus sorbet, and then to launch into his choice of grilled fillet of fresh Patagonian trout with Barbolino jus (he eats this and says it tastes suspiciously like an Alaskan salmon), roasted Black Angus beef with tomato and olive jam, prosciutto-wrapped pork medallions with dill-scented carrots, butter-roasted potatoes and green hollandaise sauce, or a baby vegetable ragout with garlic and shallots, scallion sauce and beet oil. For dessert he has the coconut custard, while everyone else at his table opts for the chocolate ice cream.

By the time dinner ends, the ship is well out in the Beagle Channel, it is 10:00 p.m., and Dr. Munn is in his stateroom exploring the various channels on his flat-screen TV. Darkness falls by 11:30 p.m. and it is time to stow everything securely in anticipation of rough seas and call it a day. Thus ends Monday, December 12. Good-bye Argentina and farewell Tierra del Fuego, the "land at the end of the world."

Drake Passage

Chapter Three
Crossing the Drake Passage

Yaw, pitch, and roll are accurate terms describing the motions of the Silver Explorer as it plows through heavy seas and 40-knot winds in the Drake Passage, notorious for turbulent seas due to the Antarctic Convergence, a natural boundary where cold polar water flows north and warmer equatorial water moves south. Where they meet, nutrients push to the surface, often attracting a multitude of seabirds and whales.

To comprehend the ship's motion, imagine a corkscrew turning slowly with you riding in the center of it. Working your way from one end to the other is possible, but requires deliberate actions. Strategically placed grab bars and handrails aid greatly as passengers such as Dr. Munn brace themselves in the shower, navigate themselves around their state rooms, and propel themselves up and down stairways.

This turning motion of the ship is useful in several ways. The light-traveling passenger interested in washing out a few articles of clothing finds that three or so inches of water in the bathtub will take on the features of a slow-action washing machine. Use soap and warm water to clean strategic parts of the garments in question, and then let them lurch underfoot from one end of the tub to the other while bathing in the shower. Stand on your knees in the shower or risk falling. When the shower is finished, lift each laundry article, rinse it in the shower, wring it out and hang it on the pull-out drying line over the tub, designed for just this purpose. How long it takes for these items to dry remains to be seen, but the ship does seem to have an excellent ventilation system.

Bodily locomotion on stairways is made interesting by the corkscrew meanderings of the vessel. As it pitches down and to the left, stair-climbers can practically float up a seven-riser flight of stairs—but to do so requires maintaining careful balance with extensive use of both handrails. Now pause at the landing as heavy gravity takes over and the ship plows up and to the right. As she rotates back, stair-climbers have another opportunity to elevate up the next set of steps, then brace themselves for the return of heavy gravity.

No land is in sight. A few birds, including the black-browed albatross, sooty shearwaters, and white-chinned petrels, glide in the air currents as they circumnavigate the ship. Gray and silver clouds obscure the eastern sun. The compass indicates a due south trajectory and the clinometer swings like a pendulum a couple degrees each side of zero—perhaps inaccurately, as this is a museum piece in the observation lounge on Deck Six where a few passengers drink coffee and wait for the 8:00 a.m. breakfast. Most remain in their cabins, cling to their mattresses, and rock gently to the hypnotic motions of the Silver Explorer.

Dr. Munn ventures out for a light, late breakfast, but finds little to calm the stomach and reduce the green around his gills except a few sips of green tea. The orange juice and eggs Benedict seem to exacerbate rather than calm the queasiness of potential seasickness.

At 10:00 a. m. it is time for Franz Bairlein of the Institute of Avian Research, Wilhelmshaven, Germany, to talk about 18 species of birds on the Antarctic Peninsula. First is the wandering albatross with its wingspan of 3 to 3.5 meters and weight of 6 to 11 kilograms. About 8,500 breeding pairs exist in the world, and while they can live for 60 years, they do not usually begin breeding until around age 13. They lay one single egg every year and both partners help with the 85-day incubation process. The young remain in the nest from 7-10 months.

The royal albatross is very similar but weighs less. Whereas the wandering albatross is mostly white with black fringes on the wings, the royal albatross has darker wings and the tip of the tail is white. A black line on the beak of the royal albatross helps distinguish it from the others.

The black-browed albatross is smaller with a two to three meter wingspan. Of the three million pairs, about 80 percent nest on the Falklands. The chicks fledge in 110 to 125 days. The grey-headed albatross has a black beak with light orange edges. The population is about 92,000 breeding pairs. The light-mantled sooty albatross has been following the ship already. Due to pollution, this species has dwindled to a population of about 20,000 pairs.

The giant petrel has also been following the ship and weighs up to five kilograms. They are doing very well and about 62,000 pairs exist. All of these birds stay in the air most of their lives by catching updrafts and rising against the wind in a pattern called dynamic soaring.

The cape petrel has a wingspan of only about a meter and with 300,000 breeding pairs, Dr. Munn can expect to see a lot of those. But it is outnumbered by the Antarctic petrel, about the same size but a slightly different wing shape and color. Four million breeding pairs of these exist.

A much smaller bird living in these waters is the Antarctic prion, a blue-grey bird with graying wings and a dark black line through the wings. There are two million breeding pairs. Also be on the lookout for the Wilson's storm petrel and black-bellied storm petrel. The legs are always longer than the tail so they're easy to spot. They always stay very close to the sea surface.

Dr. Bairlein says the penguins are the most fascinating birds, and there are five species, three of which Dr. Munn will certainly see: gentoo, chinstrap, and Adélie, the last being the most common. Seven million breeding pairs make up the chinstrap population, whereas the gentoo are in rapid decline, numbering only 320,000 pairs. Dr. Munn may also see the macaroni penguin, and possibly the emperor, but with only 220,000 pairs, these are scarce. They live on the ice shelves connected to the continent. As the duration of the sea ice becomes shorter and shorter, their environment is somewhat threatened.

Penguins are flightless, monogamous with lifelong partners, have very short legs, and reach ages of 40 to 50 years. They forage by diving as deeply as 500 meters and can remain under water for up to 20 minutes. They survive in the cold due to a very high body temperature of about 40° Celsius, and they have excellent natural insulation, plenty of body fat reserves, and metabolic adaption abilities.

These creatures are endothermic, which means their body heat is produced internally. They maintain the same body temperature regardless of the weather. Penguins have up to 90 feathers per square inch. Each individual feather is connected to a nervous system that permits it to become erect to increase insulation. They have many thousands of these feathers, and are also able to change their shape significantly to conserve heat. They can stand on ice in their bare feet due to the dramatic decrease in blood temperature from their body to the tips of their toes. A sort of heat exchanger plumbing in their legs allows returning blood to be warmed by the coming blood, which in turn is cooled by the returning blood.

The breeding biology is that the male penguin takes responsibility for the egg while the female goes to sea to fatten up. The male incubates the egg, and when it hatches the female returns and the male goes to sea, having fasted for 150 days. He has taken in zero food input during that time. At the end of his fast he weighs 20 to 25 kilos, but he doubles his weight to 45 or 50 kg by the time he must begin the next incubation period. So his life is a cycle of fattening, food storing, and fasting. He can also keep undigested food in his stomach for quite a while—and digest it as needed.

Penguins rely mainly on krill, a very tiny shrimp-like creature. Researchers have equipped the penguins with satellite transmitters to track their eating behaviors and locations. They are known to go hundreds, even thousands, of kilometers on foraging expeditions. The krill migrates vertically in the ocean—closer to the surface at night and lower during the day, and also at varying depths depending on the time of year. Penguins follow this migration by diving. An emperor penguin has been recorded diving 550 meters deep. Even the smaller penguins can go 200 meters deep. They can swim up to 10 kilometers per hour and have a very high oxygen storage capacity both in their hemoglobin (blood) as well as in their myoglobin (muscles). They also have flexible air sacs to provide ventilation and avoid decompression sickness, making it possible for them to return to the surface within a few seconds after a very deep dive. They basically "fly" underwater using their flippers.

Predator birds seeking out penguin eggs and chicks include the dark-colored southern skua and the kelp gull. Many kelp gulls swarmed around the ship yesterday in Ushuaia. Dr. Munn is also instructed to look for the snowy sheathbill that steals groceries foraged by incoming penguins. This thief looks somewhat like a white chicken. It winters in Patagonia and summers in the Southern Ocean.

When and how do these birds sleep when they are in the air? The best research so far suggests that their sleeping behavior is like that of the dolphin, where one hemisphere of the brain sleeps when another part is awake. Their total amount of sleep is probably very much like night rest, but it is hemispheric sleep.

Feeling a tad seasick, Dr. Munn elects to watch the next presentation on interactive TV in his stateroom. There he watches Dr. Peter W. Damisch present a historical summary called the "Search for the Unknown Continent." Damisch wants to put his viewers into a time machine to see the circumstances of the first polar explorers.

History suggests that Pomponius in 43 A.D. knew the earth was round because he could see the shadow of the earth on the moon during an eclipse. Scholars of that time period knew all about Europe and therefore deduced that there must be a balancing continent on the south side of the round planet. Greeks and Romans as early as 600 B.C. imagined a balance of north and south lands. They thought the equatorial zone was too hot to survive, so they went north and found how frigid things were there. They even named the imaginary people of the south the Antipodes People—people on the complete opposite side of the earth.

Damisch mentions that he doesn't read much fiction but does recommend Kim Stanley Robinson's 1998 book called *Antarctica*, a novel. He then gets back on topic to explain the astronomical constellation Ursa Major (also called the Big Bear) in the north which points to the North Star. The word "bear" in Greek is *arktos*, so in 330 B.C. they came up with the word *Ant Arktos* to define an imagined opposite bear in the southern hemisphere.

Now jump to Ferdinand Magellan who is reputed to have circumnavigated the globe from 1519 to 1522. He discovers the Straits of Magellan as a shortcut and enters the Pacific. He meets Fuegian Indians who lived mostly outside, and Magellan is impressed by them and the large number of their fires that dot the hillsides. This is why he called this the Land of Fire, *Tierra del Fuego*. Also, the Indians are larger and taller than the Europeans, so he uses the "giant" terminology of *Patagons* to describe the people of Patagonia, the giants in the land.

Did Magellan really circumnavigate the globe? No, he was killed in the Philippines. We really should remember Del Cano who brought back one of five ships and 18 crew out of the original hundreds of men. Another sailor named Anthony Pigafetta (the speaker debates whether he was a spy or a tourist), is really the first person to go all the way around the world. Pigafetta says Magellan found another strait charted by a pilot and mariner named Martin of Bohemia.

Once Spain found these southern lands, Queen Elizabeth selected Francis Drake in 1577 to break the Spanish monopoly of the area. He had already defeated some of the Spanish at sea. He set out with seven ships and 164 people and returned with just one ship. Drake saw penguins and reported killing and salting 3,000 for future food supplies. He sailed through the Magellan passage and then was hit by a hurricane that drove him far enough south that he saw open water to the east where he expected land. However, he never sailed through the passage named after him.

In 1615-16, the Dutch sailor Jacob LeMaire took two ships, the Endracht and the Hoorn, and sailed from Rotterdam to the southern tip of South America. His ships were twice the size of Drake's, but sailors too lazy to scrape barnacles off the Hoorn hull made the unfortunate mistake of trying to burn them off. They accidently burned the entire ship, leaving just the Endracht, but they named "Cape Horn" after the ship that never made it past the cape.

In the year 1700, the artist Duplessis painted Fuegian Indians of *Tierra del Fuego* depicting naked women diving for seafood. The speaker says it's no wonder sailors continued to prefer cutting through this passage rather than braving the cold waters of Drake Passage.

James Cook was the traveler to chart most of the earth mapped up to this time, and he is remembered as the first person to cross the Antarctic Circle and circumnavigate the Antarctic continent in the period from 1772-75. On three occasions he came close enough to almost see the continent, but he never actually spotted it. He got fresh water by harvesting ice and managed to reach 71° by 10 minutes south. Cook wrote about going further, "I will not say it was impossible, but will assert that the bare attempting of it would be a very dangerous enterprise, as far as I think it possible to go."

Cook was ahead of his time by figuring out that fresh food is the answer to scurvy. Sauerkraut, high in vitamin C, doesn't require refrigeration, and this colorful mix of red and green cabbage travels well. He persuaded his crew to eat it by initially serving it only to officers on the ship. This made the crew jealous, and when they finally tasted this coveted food of officers, they pretended to like the disgusting flavor. As a consequence, Cook was able to travel for an entire year with a zero death rate—unheard of at that time.

Along came William Smith in 1819, a cargo business man, owner and operator, who sailed around Cape Horn, was hit by a hurricane and driven far south until, out of the mist, he saw land where no land was known to exist. He reached 62°, 12 minutes south. To prove he saw land in this extreme southern region, he sailed down three times in the same year, and retrieved some dirt from one of the South Shetland Islands. The British authorities didn't believe him, put Bransfield in charge of his ship, and they went through what is now called the Bransfield Straits, the sea where we will sail between the islands and the Antarctic Peninsula.

Who was the first to actually sight Antarctica? It was the Russian Thaddeus Fabian Gottlieb von Bellingshausen, followed closely by Edward Bransfield, William Smith, and the American Nathaniel Palmer. So while it was probably Bellingshausen who was the first after Cook to circumnavigate and cross the Antarctic Circle, he went unrecognized because his documents were not translated out of Russian until the 1940s. He visited islands that to this day have only been visited by 25 ships.

Following the discovery of Antarctica, a massive rush of ships arrived, and within three years 98 percent of the native animals were killed as everyone came to harvest fur seals. Elephant seals were harvested for their oil. One U.K. ship took 100,000 seals that spoiled on the journey home and were sold as manure in London.

England wanted to name this region Graham's Land since he was the First Lord of the British Admiralty at the time, but the Americans wanted to name it after Nathaniel Palmer. In the 1960s, they compromised by naming part of the peninsula after each man.

Next came the explorer James Weddell who documented the seal population. He recorded the extermination of wildlife and sailed through what is now the Weddell Sea, breaking Cook's record for getting farthest south. Weddell is who named the leopard seal.

In 1838, the United States funded its first scientific expedition ever—to Antarctica. Charles Wilkes led the U.S. expedition using ships the Navy no longer wanted. After three years, Wilkes returned home but was court martialed for reasons Damisch left unexplained. Wilkes proved that it is an actual continent and not just a mass of tiny islands like Tierra del Fuego.

James Clark Ross discovered an ice shelf the size of France that today is called the Ross Ice Shelf. On 21 February 1842, they "caught" the first fish taken below the Antarctic Circle. It jumped into the boat on its own accord and was eaten by the ship's cat before anyone could dissect and study its carcass.

The lecture ends with an observation by the explorer Amundsen who said on 14 December, 1911, "Adventure is just bad planning." After the lecture, Dr. Munn goes to lunch, which consists of a mostly seafood buffet, and as he consumes a few carefully selected morsels, the captain announces that the mandatory Zodiac briefing has been postponed, since a majority of the passengers seem to be confined to their rooms by the yaw, pitch, and roll. Dr. Munn retires to his cabin for a nap to preserve energy for the 5:00 p.m. presentation by documentary photographer Richard Sidney followed by a casually elegant dinner scheduled with Captain Alexander Golubev. The sun rose on this tumultuous day at 3:57 a.m.

Seabirds follow the ship

Chapter Four
Eating His Way South

If lectures concerning Antarctica are not enough to fill the time required to cross the Drake Passage, passengers also have the option of eating in the company of others. The captain's reception is an informal affair where he introduces his crew, raises a toast to the success of the trip, and then serves dinner with choices including Maine lobster, venison, or a vegetarian plate.

Dr. Munn finds himself seated with four strangers, all of whom turn out to be American entrepreneurs who own their own businesses. Karen, who has homes in both Detroit and Maine, owns dog kennels (her favorite dog is the golden retriever) and travels extensively. To her right is a bearded gentleman from Connecticut, a dentist with a specialization in periodontics who works only on Monday, Wednesday, and Thursday.

At the end of the table sits a fellow from the northwest side of Philadelphia who owns a mold-eradication business. He recommends the mold chemical treatment product called Anabec that is a generation ahead of the competition in terms of quality and guaranteed to eradicate mold for at least five and sometimes 20 years, depending on various conditions.

Next to him sits his brother Kent, whose mother has an honorary Ph.D. from Holy Family University in Philadelphia, where Dr. Munn's grandson happens to teach. Kent now lives in South Carolina where he developed a non-medical home care network with 150 branches that he recently sold to a venture capital organization. Now at around age 50, he modestly tells people he is unemployed and enjoys spending quality time with his wife, two sons, and daughter. He plans to take one of his boys to the Galapagos Islands next year.

The caliber of conversation between these smart and successful businesspersons is fascinating, and the stories they tell keep them sitting around the table until 10:30 p.m. Of course, it is still broad daylight and they are next to the window, so nobody is aware of the hour until Kent casually mentions, "Can anyone guess how late it might be at this very moment?" Then they visit with the head waiter from Hungary for 10 minutes or so, and finally decide it is time to trundle off to bed, walking carefully as the growing swells of Antarctic waves continue corkscrewing the ship toward the bottom of the globe.

The captain cautiously approaches shelf ice

Chapter Five
South Shetland Islands

At 8:00 a.m. on December 14, Dr. Munn finds himself at Latitude 61° 24' 27" South. Longitude is 60° 36' 59" with a heading of 154°. The temperature is 1.6° Celsius, the barometric pressure stands at 996 millibars and winds are 43.2 knots at 83°. The speed of the ship appears to fluctuate between 23 knots and 12.4 knots. This is deceptive and is due to the steady rising and falling of the boat in rolling seas, but over time the speed works out to an average of 16 knots. Drake Passage is the narrowest portion of the easterly flowing Antarctic Circumpolar Current, the only place where it squeezes between land masses. When forcing itself through this 400-mile-wide bottleneck, the ocean current moves 170 million cubic yards of water per second, or roughly 800 times the flow at the mouth of the Amazon River.

Although the thermometer is barely above freezing, a brilliant sun shines through the east dining room window onto the table where Dr. Munn is consuming a normal breakfast in spite of irregular sleep. "I kept finding myself on one edge of the bed or the other," he observes, and indeed there were moments when it felt he would slide right out of bed much like an omelet in a slippery and well-oiled pan. The ship is approaching the chain of South Shetland Islands, and Dr. Munn's hope is for calmer seas once he can get between that stretch of islands and the Antarctic Peninsula.

The largest of the South Shetland Islands, King George, is home to eight different scientific stations in Antarctica. Year-round, these stations are operated by Chile, Russia, China, South Korea, Poland, Brazil, Argentina and Uruguay. Marathon runners will like to know that this island is the site of a full 26-mile course that attracts runners from around the world. However, the Silver Explorer is not interested in such a destination and heads further southwest.

The mandatory safety briefing at 10:00 a.m. begins with information regarding IAATO (International Association of Antarctic Tour Operators). This governing body controls tourism in Antarctica, a place unique for its landscape, its beauty, and its political situation. The continent is dedicated to scientific research and peaceful cooperation. Last year about 40,000 people set foot on Antarctica.

Rules of conduct are strict here. The largest wilderness area on earth, Antarctica is pristine and visitors are never permitted to drop or throw anything overboard. When on the shore, be careful to secure all belongings. Decomposition is slow in cold climates and animals can get entangled or poisoned by litter. Please inspect and clean all clothing and equipment before going ashore. Wash and disinfect boots before and after each landing. To avoid both litter and potential introduction of non-native species, IAATO members agree that food of any kind will not be taken to shore—not even gum or pills, and smoking is not permitted on the continent at all. Take away only memories and photographs. Removing anything, including rocks, feathers, bones, eggs, fossils, or anything else from the environment is strictly prohibited.

Protecting Antarctic species is rigorously enforced because the wildlife shows little fear of humans. Do not disturb the wildlife in any way. Do not feed, touch, or handle wildlife, and remember that penguins always have the right of way. There are no traffic lights! So when crossing a penguin highway, please wait as long as necessary for a gap in the traffic.

Be aware of the birds' and animals' reactions to you, and keep at least 15 feet from all wildlife. The guide will make individual-situation decisions regarding how close is appropriate. Very strict management is in place regarding where people can and cannot go. Always stay in the periphery of the rookeries of nesting birds. Avoid all molting birds and animals because they're already feeling miserable. They cannot swim during this period, and therefore they cannot eat. Just leave them in their misery!

Plants are extremely fragile, so be very careful where you walk. Damage to plants that might recover in a few months in other locations can require 10 years of recuperation in this location. Every site we visit will have guidelines for that particular area. And remember— absolutely no smoking.

Emergency refuges located in strategic spots should only be entered in the case of an emergency. The bottom

line is to stay safe. Antarctica is very unpredictable. Dress
in layers with wind-proof and water-proof outer garments.
Winds can be up to 100 knots and are frequently 30 to 70
knots. Make sure you wear your waterproof pants over the
outside of your boots so water cannot run down your pant
leg and get inside. The waterproof pants can dry in 30
minutes whereas the heavy felt liners in rubber boots can
take days to dry.

Guides will check out the safe places to walk on
glaciers. Expect slippery and uneven terrain onshore. Only
100 people are permitted ashore at a time. We are split into
four groups, and on average each group will have an hour
and a half at a time on land.

Transport between ship and shore is provided by
inflatable power boats called Zodiacs. Zodiacs are very
stable with five isolated air chambers and in an emergency
can function with two or three deflated chambers. The ship
has six smaller Zodiacs and two larger ones, which means
extras are always available for continuous shuttle runs to
deal with emergencies such as having to go to the
bathroom. No bathroom facilities are available on the
places we will visit.

Listen for announcements regarding weather, sea
conditions, landing conditions, activities, and departure
times. The mud room has a bin for each passenger where
they should always leave their rubber boots. Use the cubby
hole marked with your suite number. Use the brushes and
shower facilities to clean dirty boots.

Check the notice board on deck three to find out what
group you are in. Only two people are allowed on the
gangway at a time, and you always need both hands free for

getting into and out of the Zodiac. We always use the wrist-to-wrist sailor's grip. First place one foot onto the pontoon, then the other onto the step, and once you are in the Zodiac, sit and slide to the back of the boat. Please stay seated while the vessel is moving, lean slightly forward, and ask permission before standing to take a picture.

On arrival remain seated. The Zodiac driver will advise you, and the shore party will brief you. In the case of an emergency, you will hear a continuous long blast from the ship horn. If this should happen, go immediately back to your Zodiac for evacuation. Expect to get wet in the Zodiacs.

Following this briefing, Dr. Munn learns that an inspection of all outer-layer personal gear is to be conducted, but the event is delayed because a massive iceberg is spotted dead ahead. The captain steers within a kilometer of it so passengers can snap photos from many angles. Then the inspection resumes. Crew members carefully vacuum Velcro closures on camera packs, pick stones or sand out of boot treads, vacuum out the lint they find in Dr. Munn's new waterproof pants pockets, and generally make sure the travelers introduce no foreign substances to the region.

During lunch the announcement comes over the intercom that the Silver Explorer has made better time than expected—this Drake Passage crossing is actually one of the more placid experiences anyone could have hoped for. The ship will drop anchor near a small island between Robert Island to the west and Greenwich Island to the east in time for a landing on what from here looks like a black cobblestone beach of eroded volcanic soil. For this unscheduled stop, groups one and two must be ready to disembark by 1:30 p.m. Dr. Munn is in group three, so his group and others in group four have their chance to go ashore at 3:00 p.m.

A humpback whale is soon spotted, one of 30,000 to 40,000 worldwide. This summer visitor no doubt migrated from calving grounds off Brazil in search of a smorgasbord of seafood—mainly krill, which whales filter from the water using the bristles of 600 or so baleen plates that hang from the roofs of their mouths. A penguin playfully splashes along at portside. The ship comes to a stop and drops anchor. Dr. Munn takes pictures of Zodiacs being lowered into the water, then heads to his room to work his way into four layers of clothing in preparation for his own ride to shore on the somewhat choppy seas.

Dressed from the waist down in long johns, flannel-lined trousers, and waterproof pants pulled over his tall waterproof boots, Dr. Munn supplements this gear with three layers of upper clothing topped off with the red parka provided by Silverseas. Gloves, sunglasses, and camera complete the costume for his first step onto Antarctic soil—sort of. Actually, it's Aitcho Island (pronounced "H-O," as in Hydrographic Office, which it is named after). The black volcanic rocks and sand are covered in places with luxurious beds of mosses, so Dr. Munn is asked to stay with a group of three people and follow the hiking route marked out by ship guides.

Ten people plus the Zodiac driver power toward a small ice floe between the ship and shore. They spot five crab-eating seals basking on the ice and slow down to get a closer look. Once on shore, they deposit their lifejackets in the blue barrels and spend an hour walking quietly among rookeries of gentoo and chinstrap penguins. The earth is soiled by white and red penguin excrement thanks to their exclusive diet of krill. They build nests with a circle of small stones, and one sly gentoo sneaks about looking to steal pebbles from the neighboring nest. The neighbor sticks to the nest which contains a warm egg, but responds to the thievery with harsh squawks and aggressive beak action, so he waddles off looking for easier prey. The gentoo and chinstraps live in neighborhoods rather close to each other, but they speak different languages and seem to prefer the company of their own kind, though they can freely trudge through each other's neighborhoods on their way to open water.

Temperatures are dropping, the sun is low in the north, and Dr. Munn heads back to the blue barrels to retrieve a life jacket, scrub off his boots at one of two available scrubbing stations, and catch the next Zodiac from Aitcho Island back to the ship. There he showers off his boots, sprays them with a disinfecting agent, and leaves them in cubical 407 in the mud room.

Two nice things about this stop include the chance to walk again on terra firma, and also to walk around the ship without it swaying excessively or threatening to toss him down—or up—a stairway. No sooner is he settled back into his room when the announcement is made that he should not get too comfortable—shortly we will head back to traverse another 120 miles of open ocean in order to reach the Antarctic Peninsula. He is warned to expect six- or seven-meter swells, and is urged to again batten down the hatches of his room to keep valuables from being tossed hither and yon.

Viewing the ship from shore, surrounded by icebergs, makes a nice photo, and he can now pick out his stateroom: the fourth square window back from the bow on the starboard side, just below the fifth deck's bridge projection. The ship also features a spacious library with an internet café, boutique shopping, a full-service spa, beauty salon, fitness center, sauna, and two top-deck whirlpools which so far have not been filled because anything in them would quickly slosh over the side and into the sea. The Silver Explorer also features "the humidor," a room where connoisseurs can enjoy fine cigars and cognacs, the likes of which are offered by no other expedition ship. Next to the humidor is a dining lounge where a jolly, olive-skinned fellow smiles widely at everyone as he stabs away at the keys of an electronic keyboard housed in an elegant piano-like case.

At the 6:15 p.m. debriefing, Dr. Munn is informed he has so far covered about 560 nautical miles to reach the South Shetlands. Tomorrow he will go through Antarctic Sound and into the Weddell Sea. There he can hope to see very large tabular icebergs that calve off of ice shelves, some as long as eight miles. The hoped-for destination is Snow Hill Island, where this ship has never gone before. Reports from other ships indicate that a large gap has opened up in the frost ice and emperor penguins have been sighted! This is in the area east of James Ross Island, right on the edge of the solid pack ice. The guide has led tours for 10 years without seeing an emperor penguin, so this is an exciting possibility, but not guaranteed as the ice may close in.

The sunrise tomorrow is at 2:22 a.m., and passengers who get up at that time will see a rare quality of light and astonishing scenery (if it's not too cloudy). There is also the hope of seeing emperor penguins near Snow Hill Island. Depending on the weather, says the announcer, we may stay all day, but if not, we will take off north for the tiny pin-prick place called Devil Island with sensational views and lots of Adélie penguins. The Weddell Sea has its own weather patterns ranging from calm to 100 mile-per-hour winds.

During this announcement, the captain mentions that he generally maintains an "open bridge policy." Passengers can come to the bridge at any time to see how the ship is operated, and to get spectacular views. However, when you visit the bridge, please stay quiet. Do not disturb officers who seem to be busy, and don't push any buttons!

Now Kara explains about the six varieties of seals in this area. They include the Ross, leopard, crabeater, Weddell, elephant, and Antarctic fur seal. The Weddell seals always look happy with their upturned lips, cat-like faces, and small heads in proportion to the body. They mainly eat fish. Leopard seals have rather big necks and longer, slinkier bodies, and even their faces are rather reptilian. They are—along with the orca—the main predator in Antarctica. Note that the crabeater seal does not eat crabs—there are none down here. They eat mainly krill.

Although the various penguins stay on similar terrain, they eat in different ways and places. The chinstraps eat in shallow water; the gentoo also eat krill but further out to sea and at a different depth.

The historian explains that today is the 100th anniversary of the success of the first human being to reach the South Pole. Roald E. G. Amundsen (1872-1928) arrived there first and is one of the first persons to stay all winter in Antarctica. Amundsen was also the first to go through the Northwest Passage in 1903-06. He reached the South Pole in 99 days, arriving on December 14, 1911.

As usual, dinner is exquisite. Appetizers include liver parfait, caramelized red onion and Jarlsberg tart, or a little stew of scallops. Intermezzo can be fragrant cherry tomato consommé, peach citrus and walnut salad, or penne Arrabiata. Mango and passion fruit sorbet is then served followed by one of these entrees: Grilled fresh Patagonian sole, roasted beef with jalapeno and cilantro dressing, spring chicken, or wild mushroom and potato paté. Dessert options include a platter of cheese, dried fruit, nuts and crackers, any variety of ice creams, a milk chocolate pecan mousse, a peach tarte fine, or iced key lime cheesecake mousse. While the meals are elegant, they are served over a two-hour time period and the serving size is modest. No one goes away either hungry or too full. Dinner companions tonight include a retired investment broker and his wife from Australia, and a soon-to-retire corporate executive at American Airlines and his wife.

Almost endless tabular ice floats in the sea

Chapter Six
Weddell Sea and Snow Hill Island

This morning, the ship is surrounded by both sea ice and icebergs. Snow Hill Island off to the west is accurately named. The sheer cliff of ice at the shoreline varies in height, the lower portions about as tall as a 10-story building, the higher portions as tall as a 20-story building. Behind this sheer cliff lies a graceful line of smooth, perfect snow as far as the eye can see, both north and south. The ship works its way right up to the edge of the ice pack where an emperor penguin stands as if in greeting. Dr. Munn learns that this ship has never been able to come into this channel before due to ice, and the expedition leader is beside himself with excitement because he is seeing his first emperor penguin after 10 years of serving on this ship.

All guests are invited to go on a Zodiac tour to get closer to the wildlife. By 9:30 a.m. Dr. Munn finds himself in the company of just five other passengers and Peter the historian who steers them up close to a leopard seal, then to a few crabeater seals, and finally to yet another emperor penguin in the company of some Adélie penguins. Next, he pulls into an ice cove, all the Zodiacs turn off their engines, and for several minutes they sit in the vast silence, listening

to the quiet lapping of the waves, and the occasional splash
of a seal or penguin entering or leaving the water. After an
hour and a half of frolicking in the endlessly changing
landscape, the group returns to the ship and others get the
chance to go exploring.

This journey truly is an Antarctic expedition. The ship
goes where the expedition leaders indicate, and proof of
this conviction is the fact that neither of the destinations
reached so far were mentioned in the itinerary, and getting
this far south in the Weddell Sea was not deemed possible
as recently as a week ago. Peter the historian says, "We
shouldn't be surprised if in 10 minutes' time winds of 100
mph come swooping over Snow Hill Island and we will be
compelled to hightail it out of here." But now it is noon, the
sky is a vivid blue and white, and some Zodiacs are still out
exploring. The sun seems to be surprisingly high in the
north considering that it barely gets below the horizon in
the Southern Hemisphere. With the sunrise at 2:22 a.m. and
the sunset at 11:55 p.m., that leaves only three or so hours
of "night" which actually is not dark at all, for this is a
world of white and reflected light. The Silver Explorer is in
a place it has never been before and may never be able to
reach again, so they are making the most of it.

Peering out the window during lunch, Dr. Munn
announces that members of the Zodiac crew are up to
something. They have gotten out of their boats and are
walking on the treacherous sea ice! They are putting flags
out in a large rectangular area, the ship is maneuvering
itself right up to the edge and actually into this flow of ice,
and a couple other Zodiacs are pushing a small chunk of
sea ice out to sea, away from the ship.

Soon the announcement is made that passengers interested in actually stepping out and walking around on the flat sea ice are invited to come aboard a Zodiac. Definitely interested, Dr. Munn is on the very first transport and soon steps onto that floating world where the "snow" is more like fluffy ice crystals loosely packed so that he sinks half way up to his knees in this damp slush as he tries to walk. The position affords a great place to get a photo of the ship, the front half of which appears stuck in the massive ice field, yet Zodiacs are operating out of the back half to give passengers this rare experience.

"This is only the third time in my ten-year career that I have done this," affirms expedition director Robin West. We seem to be making all sorts of history, as this is the third time in a 24-hour period that passengers have the opportunity for Zodiac adventures away from the ship.

By 4:00 p.m. everyone is back on board, and as we have reached the southern-most reaches of the open water, the time has come to abandon the ice pack of the Snow Hill Island side of the Weddell Sea and head north to regain the tip of the Antarctic Peninsula. But on the return trip the weather is so spectacular the captain announces he will do some "tabular iceberg cruising"—swinging somewhat eastward to locate the best of the 'bergs.

White birds called Arctic terns swoop near the ship, and Franz explains that these are indeed Arctic, not Antarctic terns, and they are not lost. They are to be seen at both poles and have migrated here for this season of year.

The water is mirror-smooth. The ship slices its way north, carefully avoiding the massive tabular icebergs, but occasionally coming extremely close to the smaller floating ice. The sky remains mostly clear, and the sun is so bright it is difficult to see what is in the camera display. Crew members keep saying, "We don't often see such remarkable weather." Robin West comes on the broadcast system to announce a cocktail party on the stern at 6:45 p.m. instead of the usual debriefing in the theatre. "We must make the most of every minute of this spectacular day," he explains.

In fact, just about everybody is already on that deck enjoying the scenery, but Dr. Munn heads back to his cabin to swap batteries out of his camera and to read sections of the tour book pertaining to this area. Then he bounds back up the steps to Deck Six. "Today is the day the Lord has made," he intones. "Let us rejoice and be glad in it."

It turns out that, upon request, you can get a very nice mug of non-alcoholic hot chocolate at this cocktail party, and it is worth drinking to help reduce the impact of steadily dropping temperatures, for it was about 50° Fahrenheit out there on the snow field this afternoon. But now Dr. Munn is seeing something even more breathtaking, for right there—just next to the ship—stands an iceberg tall as a 10-story building and easily a mile long. And when we reach the end and turn the corner, behold! The massive slab of snow shelf is also a mile wide. Because it bobs in the water like an ice cube—mostly submerged—it is in fact seven or eight times thicker than the 100-foot-tall wall of densely packed snow we see projecting above the water.

The captain veers slightly east from the Snow Hill Island shore and makes these icebergs a destination in their own right. So Dr. Munn shoots another round of photos, drinks his chocolate, and then heads down to dinner.

Meanwhile, seven rare Antarctic petrels dive and swoop around the back of the ship. Astonishingly fast, it is almost impossible to photograph them in flight.

Tonight at dinner, he is seated next to Sarah who has been married to Jim for more than 50 years, and who has survived nine neurosurgeries and various other treatments for 11 metastases in the brain and 200 more throughout her body as a result of melanoma. A guinea pig for various trial treatments starting back in 2005, she is grateful to be part of the trials—otherwise her medications would cost $100,000 every three months. Although she is now blind in one eye and exhibits multiple sclerosis-type symptoms, she relishes this journey and enthusiastically makes the Zodiac trips with help from her husband and gracious staff attention.

Jim, her husband, is a professor of medicine at Stanford University where he and Sarah met long ago. He spent eight years at Johns Hopkins University in Baltimore where he acquired his doctorate degree, and in fact was alumnus of the year in 2011 in partial recognition for having funded an endowed chair for medicine. The way he tends to Sarah and her needs is a beautiful thing to watch.

Next to Jim sits Don, a British entrepreneur who likes to call himself a truck driver—he owns a company with 40 trucks and makes deliveries throughout Europe. He moved to Spain 12 years ago when his wife, Sue, quit her leadership position as a former director of an automotive parts company in England that she guided through three mergers and then retired to do the office work for her husband's company.

The dinner conversation is as good as the food, and the food is exquisite. One of Dr. Munn's companions selects a typical meal: mushroom soup with onions, leeks, and thyme, a blue cheese and pear salad with cashews and chives, a sorbet of kalamansi & lemon, and a baked fillet of fresh merluza containing creamy leeks, crispy bacon-parsley sauce, and coarse rock salt. The fancy forest berry basket dessert tops off the evening, and although it is broad daylight at 10:15 p.m., it's time for bed because of a 4:30 a.m. wakeup call—crash—we just hit another "growler," a clear, floating block of very dense ice named growler because of the way you can feel and hear it scraping past the side of the ship.

Why the early wakeup call? We hope to arrive around midnight at Brown Bluff on the western shore of the Antarctic Peninsula where we can set foot on the actual continent for the first time. Brown Bluff is a towering rust-colored and ice-capped, flat-topped mountain 2,200 feet high on the Antarctic continent and home to Adélie and gentoo penguins—some 250,000 of them. Birds such as the all-white snow petrels and skuas should be swooping around as well. Dr. Munn is advised to expect a wet landing, and once ashore may have the opportunity to take a guided walk up a glacier—unless the inclement weather gets there before he does.

Solid in winter, liquid in summer

Chapter Seven
Antarctic Passage

The expedition director awakens everyone at 4:30 a.m. on December 16 with a loud announcement that the shore excursion to Brown Bluff must be cancelled due to winds in excess of 30 mph and waves going directly toward land making it impossible to navigate with the Zodiacs. Therefore, the ship will pull up anchor and head for tomorrow's destination—yet to be unveiled. Brown Bluff, its creeping glacier, and its massive population of Adélie penguins will have to wait for another day to get visitors.

Adélie penguins have 38 colonies with a population of more than five million in the Ross Sea region, half-a-million of them on Ross Island. They lay two eggs that incubate for about 33 days and the chicks remain in the nest for 22 days. The chicks molt into their juvenile plumage and go out to sea after about 50 or 60 days. These are the "tuxedo" penguins with tails a little longer than other penguins' tails. They can swim up to 45 miles per hour in their tuxedos and always wear these dinner jackets while feeding on Antarctic krill, ice krill, and silverfish.

Seasoned travelers, the Adélie penguins migrate an average of about 13,000 kilometers each year as they follow the sun from their breeding colonies to winter foraging grounds and back again. The longest treks have been recorded at 17,600 kilometers.

After a couple more hours of shut-eye, Dr. Munn pays a visit to the bridge where four crew members are on duty. Quietly the captain says to the midshipman, "328."

"Click, click, click" go the little dials.

"328," replies the midshipman.

To his right the navigator reaches to the ceiling, switches a knob, and a massive windshield wiper squeegees rain from the giant windscreen. He continually peers ahead through his binoculars. Giant tabular icebergs left, right, and dead ahead appear on the radar as well as to the naked eye.

"324," says the captain.

The midshipman's fingers turn three little black nobs. "Click, click, click."

"324," says the midshipman. The ship twists a tad farther to the south.

By 7:00 a.m. winds have risen to 72 mph, just shy of hurricane force. The temperature is 37° Fahrenheit, but standing outside on deck is nearly impossible. The floor is wet, the wind is powerful in its own right, and when it comes around the corner of the bow it is enough to knock a man over. Going ashore at Brown Bluff would have been catastrophic in these conditions and expedition leaders are prudent to head for the western shores of the Antarctic Peninsula which is sheltered by outlying islands.

The ship is steadily turning left to begin working its way down the western shore of the peninsula. Passengers are nowhere to be seen, but one fellow stands in the observation lounge drinking orange juice and dressed in a freshly laundered set of clothes and a t-shirt that reads, "This is what a really cool Grandpa looks like."

The ship is no longer cork-screwing forward as it did on the Drake Passage. It is rising and falling front to back and very easy to walk around on, and it is possible to actually stand up in the shower and not get capsized.

Exploring the storehouses of snow

Chapter Eight
Meet the Krill

Krill live under these waters where Dr. Munn's vessel plunges southward. Krill are the most important animal in Antarctica because they are at the bottom of the food chain and support all other animal life out here. Not until the 1980s did scientists begin to study krill in this part of the world. These tiny shrimp-like organisms have antennas, compound eyes, a gastric mill, hepatopancreas, gut, gills, ice rakes up front, and swimming legs at the back.

Krill are beautifully translucent but have an overall red tint and big black eyes that pop out like smooth mushrooms, and they can look greenish because of the plankton they eat. *Euphausia superba* is the species of the most common krill of the 12 varieties in this part of the world. Their size is about 6.35 centimeters, their lifespan is from five to nine years (assuming they are not eaten), and they reach sexual maturity in three years. The population has to be guessed, but scientists calculate something around 6,500 million metric tons of these critters distributed all the way around the Antarctic Continent, but they are concentrated here in the waters of the Antarctic Peninsula. Researchers measure the population partly by knowing how much krill various other animals need to eat to survive, count the numbers of those easier-to-count animals, and then do the math to get a minimum count of the number of krill eaten over a certain time period in a particular area.

Krill swarms are now being studied, and they are distinct units. You can have 30,000 krill per cubic meter of water with small units within—clusters of males here, females there, and juveniles in another school. Krill should not be called plankton, but rather neckton, because they have the ability to move against the current. They sort of gallop in the water and can also move like a shrimp with a humping motion. They can move at eight times their body length per second, or with the abdomen-flex up to 11 times their body length per second. In eight days one krill swarm was clocked moving 45 nautical miles against the current, so they can be really mobile. The feces of krill sink to the bottom of the ocean floor which sequesters carbon down there and fertilizes the ocean floor—different from whale poop. Whales tend to poop at the surface, the poop floats, and that adds to the nutrient level at the surface of the ocean.

Krill begin life as an egg that sinks 300-400 meters deep, hatches down there, and then morphs through three stages until they return to the surface as juvenile krill and spend the winter under the ice. Plankton grows on the bottom side of the sea ice and it makes a perfect environment for krill, which scrape the algae and other organisms off the ice from the underside—they can clear a one-foot square area in 10 minutes. They molt, as they grow a new exoskeleton every 20 days. They can even molt spontaneously, such as when they are being attacked—shed the exoskeleton and zip out of there, hoping the predator is fooled and eats the empty shell instead of the escaped krill.

Krill are mostly vegetarian, but they are also predators of other organisms smaller than they are. They also reproduce prolifically: A ripe ovary can be 1/3 the size of a female's overall body weight, and she can release up to 20,000 eggs per season.

Life at the bottom of the food chain is precarious, for quite a number of other species depend on krill for survival: Cape petrels rely on krill. Crabeater seals, the largest and most numerous seals on earth, eat krill. They dive 50 to 80 meters deep to feed and consume 15 kg of krill a day. Antarctic fur seals eat krill. Half of the leopard seals' diet is krill, but they also eat other seals and penguins. The Antarctic minke are fairly small whales that eat krill. Like all baleen whales they gulp water, trap prey inside their mouths, and eject the water but trap the food, which they swallow. Humpback whales eat krill.

Adélie penguins eat krill. Chinstrap penguins eat krill. Ice fish eat krill. Salpa are jellyfish-looking things that live about a year. They have doubled in population over the last decade and the krill population has gone down measurably, so no doubt they also eat krill. And finally, people eat krill. They are quite good, but rather small and tiresome to clean. Mostly, krill is used for Omega-3 krill oil for humans, or as food for fish farms.

Zodiac transport

Chapter Nine
The Southern Ocean

The Southern Ocean begins at 60° south and extends all the way around the South Pole. It is our newest ocean both politically and geographically. Politically, it was created in the year 2000. Geographically, it was created 30 or 40 million years ago when Antarctica broke away from South America.

Biologically, by looking at the distribution of animals, the Southern Ocean can be defined by the Polar Front or Antarctic Convergence, where the very cold Antarctic waters extend quite a ways further north than 60°, basically to the tip of Argentina/Chile. The animals living south of the Polar Front have adapted to an extreme condition and do not do well above the Polar Front. Also, of course, animals from warmer climates cannot survive in this colder region.

The Polar Front is difficult to measure because it fluctuates throughout the year by as much as 100 miles. Interestingly, cold water contains more life than warm water because it increases the concentration of potential dissolved oxygen. Colder molecules don't move around as much and therefore can contain more oxygen as well as more nutrients brought up from the ocean floor during the upwelling as deep water approaches the Antarctic Continent.

In the summer, this region morphs into four million square kilometers of floating ice. Autumn freezes an average of 5.75 square kilometers per minute. In winter 19 million square kilometers of ice is produced and it's about one to two meters thick. Krill depend on this ice for their development.[1]

Sea ice pushes out the salt as it freezes, and this salt accumulates immediately under the ice and then sinks, thus kick-starting the major ocean currents. Salt also brings greenhouse gases down with it where it stays for a long time. Basically this is a marine eco-system (the largest land animal is a wingless fly!), but in the marine eco-system, the larger the animal is, the easier it is able to survive in the cold. The creatures need lots of feathers and lots of fat for insulation, and it also helps to have a long life expectancy. Biodiversity drops dramatically as you approach the poles, but the population size of each species increases dramatically as you approach the poles. Life span also tends to increase, and this is necessary for survival in a harsh environment.

---

[1] If you are annoyed by the fluctuating units of measure, note that the expedition staff is from all over the world including England, Australia, South Africa, Germany, Argentina, and the United States. They all use their own units of measure, and this writer has simply recorded what they said.

About 75 percent of the Antarctic fish are in the same order of species. The tooth fish and the ice fish are tasty. The ice fish has a ghostly glow and contains no red blood cells—zero hemoglobin—total freaks of nature. No other vertebrate shows this "adaptation." The way they get around is by taking oxygen right through the skin directly into their circulatory system. They have huge arteries, veins, and hearts.

Two terrestrial birds of Antarctica, the sheath bill, and the black-faced sheath bill, are really part of the marine environment. Albatrosses are the largest flying birds in the world and come into this area just to forage, and then breed elsewhere. Petrels have tube noses, a tube on top of the upper beak—and that is all they have in common. The various petrels range from very small to gigantic. They basically smell out their environment. They can tell the difference in smell between their nest and their neighbor's nest, their mate and their neighbor's mate, their chick with their neighbor's chick. They can also smell their way back home after ranging thousands of miles over the ocean.

There's only one gull in all of Antarctica—the kelp gull.

The Arctic tern flies here to escape winter and then migrates back north. The Antarctic tern are subtly different in looks but this is their home. They are a sea bird but only plunge into the water to get food. They have tiny orange feet and lay an egg that is very hard to see because it is so well camouflaged.

Cormorants lay up to three eggs, eat fish and squid caught by diving, and they exist in three types distinguished by where the white line meets the face—but basically they're all blue-eyed cormorants.

Penguins come in 17 species worldwide, four breeding on this continent, one breeding in austral winter. Scientists estimate there could have been 42 varieties of penguins millions of years ago, the largest one being about five feet tall.

Six species of seal live in this region. This expedition has seen three and may see an elephant seal, but the fur seal won't arrive in this region until after we leave. We will not see the Ross seal because it lives much farther south and is incredibly rare.

Elephant seals can dive a mile deep because their arteries and veins are packed with cholesterol, which keeps them open from the excessive pressure at those depths. The only real difference between a whale and a seal is that the whale never needs to come to land or ice for any reason. Whales do everything in the water, and there are no specifically Antarctic species, but rather global wanderers who come here during the Antarctic summer for feeding in the rich waters of the Southern Ocean.

Visitors to this region generally can see the humpback whales that show their tail, the minke whale that are small and usually pop their nose up first when they come to the surface, and the orca, the largest of the dolphin/porpoise group, distinguished by their tall tail fin.

The Southern Ocean lectures go a long way to explain why in this region there are a great many of only a few species of wildlife. Meanwhile, out in the observation lounge the paraphernalia for a Jewish worship service is set up, which raises an interesting question for Dr. Munn to ponder: If the Sabbath begins on Friday at sundown, what do you do this far south when the sun sets after midnight? Perhaps they have arbitrarily set a time on Friday evening that transcends the biblical injunction. A Seventh Day Adventist overhears this conversation and mentions their solution: make the religious observance begin at the same time every Friday night. It meets the spirit of the law and allows for better planning in a modern world that follows a clock rather than the sun.

To summarize today's progress, the ship started the morning in the Antarctic Sound, pulled well out into the Bransfield Strait, and headed south by southwest down the shore of the Antarctic Peninsula. By now, 4:45 p.m., the second of two small islands appears on the left, and we continue to plunge forward toward Gerlache Strait. The tour director indicates that the destination is Neko Harbour in Graham Land of the Antarctic Peninsula, tucked into the lee of Anvers Island. Who can say what the wind and temperature may be? But at least the seas should be calm in this well-protected place where on Saturday we hope to make our first landfall on the actual soil of Antarctica.

The sheer ice cliffs lining the coast in Neko Harbour are broken by a tiny rocky point where gentoo penguins nest in an area well up the slope. Further yet up the hill resides a skua nesting ground, and they should be respected, for they are predators and as likely to stab a hole in your skull as to flee from your advances.

Neko Harbour is named after the whaling factory ship that often operated in this bay between 1911 and 1924. The foundation of a small wooden hut just above the beach was an emergency shelter built by the Argentinian Antarctic

Program, but a storm blew it away a few years ago and now penguins nest on the old concrete slab. The exact location is 64° by 50'S, 62° by 33'W.

This day at sea has kept most passengers out of sight. Only a handful appeared at breakfast, maybe a few dozen at lunch, and 20 or 30 for the lectures. At 4:00 p.m. Dr. Munn heads to high tea where he enjoys a variety of pastries and tiny sandwich and cookie delicacies, an exotic tea, and further conversation with the father of the Seventh Day Adventist gentleman from Minnesota who says his company has poured every cubic foot of cement used to build the Mayo Clinic. The cement man's son looks like Jay Leno. His daughter and niece are traveling with him. It helps to not jump to conclusions when meeting new people, for it turns out that the Leno-looking man, suspected a few days ago of having a trophy wife, turns out to have a daughter! She spent last year in Ethiopia doing missions work and is now a graduate student in communications at Andrews University in Michigan.

As the ship approaches Neko Harbour through Gerlache Strait, it is worth learning a bit of history. Adrien de Gerlache led the Belgica expedition of 1897-99. This party of 19 men was the first to winter in the Peninsula region, surviving for 13 months on their ship after it became locked in ice. Fortunately for them, one of these men was the American Frederick Cook, a doctor and one of those gifted people able to help hold morale together for these sailors from many different countries. The third mate was Norwegian Roald Amundsen who later distinguished himself as the most successful polar explorer, the first to later reach the South Pole.

Humpback whales are frequently found in Gerlache Strait, and all passengers are encouraged to dress warmly, stand outside, and keep a sharp eye out for the dark back and bushy snout of a feeding humpback. Passengers may also get a glimpse of the fast-swimming minke and killer whales (orcas).

The Southern Sea is full of life, and also full of ice. The glacier expert mentions that less than three percent of the water in the world is fresh; the rest is salt water. Of the three percent, less that 30 percent of that is liquid. The remaining 69 percent is locked up in glaciers. Recent radar research in Antarctica reveals many previously unknown mountain ranges as big as the Alps. Some of the mountains of Antarctica are called "Nunataks," island mountains entirely surrounded by glacier ice. Many mountains of today were Nunataks in the past.

The Antarctic continent on average is covered with ice three miles deep. Ice core samples measuring the composition of the atmosphere locked into the ice have charted the history of Antarctica going back 1.5 million years. Using similar techniques in Greenland, scientists were able to find the level corresponding with the Chernobyl nuclear accident, and going on from there they can identify and date strategic weather and geological events in history.

Antarctica is the coldest, windiest, driest continent in the world. How can it be the driest? If you take into account the surface of the ice sheet, the average altitude is 2,500 feet. If you remove the ice, it is the lowest continent on earth, but 99.7 percent is ice-covered.

At the daily briefing, Robin West says yesterday was such a truly phenomenal day that Richard has already put together a short documentary video. Passengers watch it on the big screen in the auditorium, and less than 30 seconds into the program Dr. Munn says, "I'm buying one." Indeed, it is a spectacular and very accurate report of what he saw and did.

Here is tomorrow's plan: After going to Neko Harbour in the morning, we will go back up to Cuverville Island in the afternoon, taking a shortcut where we hope to see seals on the ice. West shows photos of what we can expect to do in the morning, which includes a walk in the snow that ends in a steep snow slide that drops adventuresome passengers all the way down the hill back to the shore. What takes 20 minutes to climb takes 30 seconds to descend.

Cuverville Island in the afternoon is an enjoyable place to come ashore and just sit down to observe wildlife and deep snow. Energetic types can climb as far as they feel comfortable on the bluff. Deep snow makes this climb both challenging and fascinating.

Penguin highways are all over this place—little roads in the snow where penguins navigate between their nests and the sea. Humans should avoid these and note that penguins always have the right of way. There are no guides at Cuverville, just some designated areas where visitors should not walk.

John Wesley reaches the seventh continent

Chapter Ten
Antarctica

On Saturday, December 17, 2011, Dr. Munn steps out of the Zodiac at Neko Harbour onto the actual Antarctic Peninsula, finally achieving his lifelong dream that inspired this journey. The sky is an intense blue, dotted with partly cloudy patches of white and a dazzling sun in the north. The temperature is 34° Fahrenheit.

The Zodiac ride from ship to shore includes a one-hour side-trip to see how close it can get to a humpback whale lurking in the harbor. Dr. Munn gets as close as is comfortable. The possibility that this beast could rise under the Zodiac and dump everyone out enters the imagination of many passengers. They see the whale's head, his humpback, his dorsal fin, and his massive tail. Dr. Munn spends his time trying to get pictures, then his Zodiac cruises over to the landing site where ship crew members have plowed a path through the floating ice to shore.

On a mission for Jay Mansur of Asbury Theological Seminary, Dr. Munn does not fail to take a stuffed doll of John Wesley carrying a Bible to the end of the world with him. A long-standing board member of the Seminary, Dr.

Munn snaps a few photos of Wesley for the amusement of his colleagues at Asbury.

Dr. Munn hikes a good way uphill at Neko Harbour, past a sleeping seal and a colony of penguins. On his left a glacier pushes ever seaward; on his right rises a smooth, snow-covered hill. From the top of this rise he takes stunning photographs of the harbor, the ship, the mountains, and the endless storehouses of snow.

At noon, passengers return to the ship and eat lunch while the vessel repositions to Cuverville Island, a rookery for gentoo penguins and a 1,000-foot-high, snow-covered hill that about 50 passengers climb in a one-hour assault. The climb involves walking at a steady upward incline over deep snow and creating switchbacks until attaining the summit where a group photo is taken and people sit down in the white fluff and just gaze about themselves, trying to take in the grandeur of gigantic, snow-covered mountains, pristine water in the ocean below, and the vivid white light that causes so much confusion for auto-focus cameras that can't seem to measure distance amidst all these levels of whiteness. Vast, vast storehouses of snow!

It takes a bit less than an hour on the return trip down the mountain, followed by the usual Zodiac ride, boot-washing ceremony, shower, supper, and bedtime. During this time the ship has moved once again and is now anchored at Port Lockroy, a natural harbor located on the western side of Wiencke Island in the Palmer Archipelago. After its discovery in 1903, it was used mainly by whalers. In February 1944, the British established "Base A" on Goudlier Island, the earliest example of a British scientific research station in the Antarctic Peninsula.

These days Port Lockroy is operated as a living museum by the United Kingdom. A fairly small, low-lying island, they permit no more than 60 people ashore at any given time, and no more than 35 can be inside the base at a time. Visitors are permitted to roam around freely, but must stay on the paths and not go into the roped-off areas where a research project is being carried out to determine the impact of humans on the penguin population. The roped-off area contains the control group of penguins that are not permitted to have human contact.

Ship personnel assume passengers will want a Port Lockroy stamp in their passport, and they will automatically do this unless requested not to. All passports were collected by the front office upon entrance to the ship, so ship personnel automatically take care of this detail.

The landing involves stepping off the front of the Zodiac onto a rock cliff. At the top of the cliff awaits a shopping opportunity where we are told some passengers on a Chinese charter ship last year spent $30,000 in one day, setting a record for the little shop. This is the place to buy the best maps of Antarctica, some good books, and to look at an informative museum. There is also a post office where visitors can buy a card and stamps, write notes, and mail them. The post card will go to the Falkland Islands on the next ship, then to London on the weekly military flight, and from there to its final destination.

The plan for Sunday afternoon is to head into Lemaire Channel, passing between 3,000-foot-high mountains on both sides of the ship. Then the plan is to either go north passing Pleaneau Island, or south to Peterman Island. If the southern route is filled with ice and the ship can't get through, it may have to do a U-turn and send passengers whale hunting in the Zodiacs.

At the usual briefing that evening, bird expert Franz reports that 2011 recorded the first loss of an emperor penguin colony in the recent period of Antarctic regional warming. Implications for the other colonies are being studied. The population had declined from 6,000 pairs in 1960 to 2,500 in 2000.

The historian then reports that Port Lockroy was discovered in February 1904 by a French expedition. In the 1940s, Ernest-Felix Kruder of Germany captured the entire Norwegian whaling fleet and reduced the production of whale oil from huge quantities to zero. The English response from 1943-45 was to establish a coast-watching operation, and at the same time scientists hitched a ride to study the area. The research was carried out from 1944-62, and the site served as a research station for the British government. They picked Port Lockroy because at that time it had no penguins. Ironically, the penguins have adopted the island now and Dr. Munn sees scores of them. In the 1980s, penguins colonized Goudier. In 1994, the island was designated a historic site. And in 1996, the facilities were renovated and turned into what it is today.

Upon returning to his stateroom after dinner, Dr. Munn finds an impressive certificate awaiting his attention. A picture of the ship graces the top, scenery and Antarctic wildlife decorate the margins, and the text reads as follows:

Proclamation
*I, Australis Rex, Ruler of the Southern Winds
and Sovereign*

Of all the frozen Reaches it touches,
do solemnly Declare that
Harold Munn
Did by My Royal Consent pass the gateway to the
bottom of the world
At Neko Harbour on the 17th of December, 2011
Aboard the MS Silver Explorer
In latitude 64.50'S and longitude 62.31'W
And enter the Southernmost Reaches of my vast realm
by Setting Foot Upon
The Great White Continent's Antarctic Peninsula.
We declare him a Loyal Member of the Most Ancient Order
of the Rednose and do call upon all icebergs, Sea Lions,
Penguins, Whales, Mermaidens, Seals and other Denizens
of those Frigid Deeps to show him due respect or incur my
Royal Displeasure.
Captain: Alexander Golubev
Expedition Leader: Robin West
Signed: Australis Rex
Ruler of the Southern Winds

Plowing through the Lamaire Channel

Chapter Eleven
Breaking the Ice

Around midnight at the beginning of Sunday, December 18—not actual night for the sun has just set and it is very light—the sea was smooth glass. Not smooth *like* glass, but extremely smooth and with a very, very thin freezing surface on top—smooth glass! At 8:00 a.m. Dr. Munn takes the Zodiac to Port Lockroy to buy and mail a postcard for his wife, visit the small museum, and have a look at the evidence left by whalers who filled this port the first half of the twentieth century. He is particularly interested in the half-mile-long snowdrift atop the adjacent point that in earlier times served as a landing strip for airplanes. Dr. Munn then catches the next Zodiac on to Jougla Point, a destination nearby where he can look at whale skeletons, gentoo penguins, and blue-eyed shags. He also gets an up-close look at pairs of nesting cormorants. The place is wet and muddy.

The cost of mailing a postcard from here is one American dollar, and the card will travel via the next ship going to the Falkland Islands—there is one every week—and the next one is tomorrow. From there the letter is taken on the weekly military transport flight to the United

Kingdom and then mailed to its destination anywhere in the world. No doubt most passengers will have been home for a week or two before their postcards arrive at their destinations. For this reason, the cards may contain more humor than news. One passenger reportedly suggested writing to an acquaintance in the civilized world that food here is scarce, the weather closing in, the last of the sled dogs is dead, and he despairs of life.

Gallows humor in such a formidable place brings to mind the reality that, although it is Sunday, there is no official sense in which any Creator is acknowledged by the scientific crew. During a snow climb yesterday one expedition leader was innocently asked by a hiker, "As you marvel at this amazing landscape and the miracle of life that thrives here, do you ever wonder whether there is any possibility of intelligent design to this place?"

"No!" she scoffed, "I don't need that." The hiker behind her added emphatically, "If there was a creator, he would have to be an idiot to make such a place as this!"

Which brings to mind the Scripture text for today, Psalm 10:4: "In the pride of his face the wicked does not seek him; all his thoughts are, 'There is no God.'"

For a New Testament reading consider Romans 1:18-22: "The wrath of God is revealed from heaven against all ungodliness and unrighteousness of men, who by their unrighteousness suppress the truth. For what can be known about God is plain to them, because God has shown it to them. For his invisible attributes, namely, his eternal power and divine nature, have been clearly perceived, ever since the creation of the world, in the things that have been made. So they are without excuse. For although they knew God, they did not honor him as God or give thanks to him, but they became futile in their thinking and their foolish hearts were darkened. Claiming to be wise, they became fools."

An interesting thing to wonder about is whether two persons standing side by side at the bow of the ship gazing into the storehouses of snow may be doing opposite things: one sinning with impunity, the other worshiping profoundly, for one is bowing down to the creation and thinking, "Wow, what a spectacular evolutionary process that over millions of years has accidently produced such a remarkable environment!" The other may tremble in amazement and cry out in his heart, "Who can know the mind of God? How magnificent are his ways; his thoughts beyond finding out; his power beyond comprehension. How great—how great!—is our God!"

By 11:30 this morning the last Zodiac returns to the ship and passengers are urged to grab an early lunch and be on deck by 1:00 p.m. to experience an attempted passage through the very dramatic and scenic Lamaire Channel, a narrow passage between a tall mountain island on the right and a tall mainland mountain on the left. By 2:00 p.m. the ship is well into the and channel passengers are able to spot a dense pack of floating ice completely blocking the planned route. The captain approaches the ice, pauses maybe 100 feet away, and maneuvers for about 15 minutes before plunging ahead.

The Silver Explorer is able to cut through broken ice five or six feet thick as long as there is somewhere to push the ice mass, but it is not an ice breaker capable of busting through solid ice. This explains why the ship is able to plow perhaps a half-mile into the field of ice, but the channel steadily narrows, the ice becomes thicker and thicker with nowhere to go, and ultimately the captain decides to make a U-turn. Meanwhile, passengers packing the bow of the ship are fascinated by the attempt, and nobody seems disappointed that Zodiac tours are being cancelled for the afternoon due to very high winds, increasingly inclement weather, and frankly not much to look at that they can't see as well or better from the ship.

Up on the bridge the expedition leader studies charts, discusses options with the captain, and then announces a decision to head for Paradise Bay on the Antarctic Peninsula, about 25 nautical miles away. A ship tour of the bay (no Zodiacs) should reveal spectacular mountains, glaciers, and icebergs, and possibly crabeater seals and minke whales. From the ship, passengers will also be able to observe Argentina's Almirante Brown Research Station.

Paradise Bay was given this name for a reason. Glacier-covered mountains reflect their grandeur in the smooth water, cormorants nesting on rocky cliffs soar overhead and swoop down to the water, and floating ice and icebergs reflect every shade of blue in the spectrum. The ship passes close to the abandoned Argentine research station as well as an active outpost manned by Chileans.

At 6:00 p.m. exciting news is broadcast: Passengers are invited to do Zodiac tours of Paradise Bay after all; another ship scheduled for this time cannot arrive due to heavy seas. Hence, at 7:30 p.m. Dr. Munn finds himself again stepping into a Zodiac for his eighth destination in a little black inflatable rubber boat. He gets up-close looks at nesting cormorants, a Weddell seal rubbing its flippers together, curling up its tail, and scratching itself while drifting about on a small iceberg, and a skua on a small piece of ice pecking away at a carcass of what may have been a juvenile snow petrel. A massive, rugged, translucent ice sculpture reflecting emerald and blackish green shades floats nearby—another "growler," so named because of the terrific noise they make when run over by the ice-hull ship.

Dinner is very late tonight—9:00 p.m., and around 10:00 p.m. word comes that Dr. Munn can expect to arrive at Whalers Bay in Deception Island around 8:00 a.m. on Monday. "In" Deception Island is as accurate as "on" because the island forms an almost complete circle made by a not-so-old volcano that erupted most recently in 1967, 1969, and 1970. In 1829 it was the first Antarctic land mass to be accurately surveyed and in 1944 was the site of earliest science bases. This horseshoe-shaped island surrounds Port Foster, and water in the collapsed center of the volcano is 525 feet deep and between six and 10 miles across. Dr. Munn is advised to be at the bow of the ship in the morning to enjoy sailing into this caldera through the gap in the island known as Neptune's Bellows, a dramatic sight with rocky walls close to starboard and wildlife on both sides—especially chinstrap penguins and cape petrels—for this place is home to 140,000 pairs of chinstraps (that's 280,000 plus offspring).

While about 40,000 people visit the Antarctic Continent each year, some 10,000 of them stream through Deception Island—most on ships without the capacity to navigate the narrow, ice-filled bays on the mainland frequented by Dr. Munn and his erstwhile traveling companions on the Silver Explorer. Attractions at Port

Foster include huge old whale oil storage barrels, a massive rusting dry dock, odd bits of abandoned equipment, whalebones, and debris from the whaling and research period. Heat causing steam rises through the soil along the shoreline, and passengers who wish to do so are invited to take the Polar Plunge into these waters.

That night, to document the absence of darkness, Dr. Munn's travel companion finds himself climbing up to the balconies on deck six at 1:30 a.m. to take photos in all directions. For all appearances, instead of the middle of the night halfway between sunset and sunrise, it looks to be a foggy or overcast winter afternoon in Michigan. It has never been dark since leaving Argentina, and won't be until they return in the early hours of Thursday, December 22, the first day of summer.

Around 8:00 a.m., disembarkation begins for Deception Island on which are the remains of the biggest whale processing factory in Antarctica until 1931, when the population of whales was pretty well wiped out. From this location, Nathaniel Palmer became the first documented American to sight the Antarctic continent in 1820 when he stood in a giant cleft in the wall of the caldera called Neptune's Window and looked out across Bransfield Strait.

The black sand on the shore is warm to the touch and actually hot if you push down a few inches underground. Surface water is warm for maybe six inches deep in the area of the beach where heat rises through the earth from the heart of the sleeping volcano. In this location, 30 or so passengers on this expedition take the Polar Plunge, which consists of stripping down to the pre-planned swimming suit under-garment, rushing into the water until about waist deep, and diving into what turns out to be extremely cold, salty water.

The second person to go for this morning swim reports that a quick U-turn and about six powerful overhand strokes brings the "polar bare" back to knee-deep water where staff members ask for the polar-plunger's room number and wrap him in a big blue towel. He suddenly realizes he is in shock from the cold and quickly takes many deep breaths while drying off and putting on his waterproof pants and enough of his other gear to get back into a Zodiac and thence to the ship, where he lounges in one of the two aft hot tubs for a few minutes before getting a hot shower and fresh change of clothes. That evening in his state room he finds a certificate with his name emblazoned across the top and the following message:

Having successfully entered
the brisk waters of the Antarctic
At latitude 62° 58.75' S
and longitude 060° 33.65' W
On this day, the 19th of December 2011
Is hereby declared an official member of the
Silver Explorer Penguin Club

The polar plunge is the perfect ending to a morning of vigorous walking over the crumbly volcanic rock and ash that constitutes the soil of this place, and by 11:30 a.m. the ship has again pulled up anchor and headed back out through Neptune's Bellows—the narrow entry to this bay and the lowest rim of the volcanic caldera, to resume its voyage.

Bailey Head chinstrap penguins

Chapter Twelve
Penguin Paradise

As Dr. Munn sits down to lunch with David and Sharon, a Chinese couple who met in London but now live in Singapore where they are bankers and hedge fund managers, the announcement is made that—thanks to unusually calm weather—the crew will drop anchor to the east of the Deception Island entrance and send Zodiacs ashore to Baily Head, the exact home of the 140,000 breeding pairs of penguins, the largest chinstrap colony in Antarctica. Turbulent seas prevent most travelers from putting in at this location because it is right on the main channel—a perfect habitat for penguins due to the abundance of krill.

The shore is a steep bank of black pea gravel, difficult to walk in, and a very treacherous spot where previous Zodiacs have met with disaster. Dr. Munn abides judiciously by every precaution of the expert navigators and in due time emerges beyond the tide line where he is privileged to discover a single macaroni penguin lounging about with the quarter million chinstraps. A walk around the head and into a protected valley delivers him to a natural, massive amphitheater a mile or so across and absolutely swarming in a plentiful "penguinesque" panorama where some eggs hatched yesterday, many more are hatching today, and most will hatch by the first day of summer two days hence.

Patient amateur photographers with small, cheap cameras wait quietly, fire away incessantly, and manage to capture the rare view of a one-day-old penguin getting food rammed down its throat by a parent. Alternately, the parent holds its mouth open and the chick reaches its head far up inside the mouth of the adult to gulp some food.

This is Dr. Munn's 10th Zodiac destination, so he has visited precisely twice as many places as he had hoped on this voyage. Now back in his stateroom, he places a call to his wife to wish her a happy 62nd wedding anniversary. She's not home, so he'll try again in the evening.

After successfully emailing four documents that summarize recent events in his journey, Dr. Munn sits down to high tea—it is a British ship, after all—to relax and nibble cheesecake wedges, raisin and nut cookies, and tiny sandwiches with the crust trimmed off. Then he hightails it to the bridge to check the charts and ascertain the most likely route back across the Drake Passage. Astonishingly, he discovers a half-mile square tabular iceberg at ten o'clock to starboard. "Imagine running into that island of ice at night without radar!" he observes. He meant "at dark," but come to think of it, down here at this time of year there is no "dark" at night.

This final look at the western shores of Deception Island is likely the last glimpse of land he will have until the coast of Argentina comes into view two days hence. It is time to say good-bye to that final island, that final dramatic iceberg—goodbye to these two things that so concisely summarize that which is Antarctica: snow and rock in giant proportions.

At the evening recap, Robin West shows videos of attempted landings at Baily Head in which sudden huge waves wipe out Zodiacs and one in which a passenger falls overboard and is run over by the rubber dingy. Another problem is when the weather becomes worse while passengers are on shore and they are stranded. The only way out then is to hike three miles over the mountain to the lagoon inside the caldera where calmer seas make it possible for them to safely return to the ship. Everyone in attendance breathes a sigh of relief that this particular adventure did not happen to them.

Franz reports that, thanks to the spontaneous stop at Baily Head, explorers got to see a macaroni penguin and therefore have now seen all five of the varieties of penguins that live in Antarctica. Visitors generally cannot hope to see them on this expedition.

The word *penguin* is imagined by some to derive from the Welsh words *pen* (head) and *gwyn* (white). However, there are no other examples of a Welsh word becoming the basis of words throughout European languages, so maybe this is just a fanciful notion. More likely, it comes from the Latin *pinguis* (fat). The name *petrel* may derive from Saint Peter because in certain of their flight patterns petrels appear to be walking on water.

The next speaker is explaining that the prime meridian goes from the South Pole to England, and therefore the map is always drawn with the Antarctic Peninsula off to the left and pointing "northwest" even though every direction is north from the pole. A temperature of -129° Fahrenheit, the coldest temperature ever recorded, was detected on this coldest continent in the world in the 1980s.

Antarctica doubles its size every winter if you include all the sea ice and snow that accumulate by the end of the season. Everywhere Dr. Munn has sailed since his arrival at the South Shetland Islands is solid ice in July.

Kara points out that west and east Antarctica are very different. West Antarctica is really a lot of mountainous islands united by a massive ice shelf making it look like one piece of land, whereas east Antarctica is a land mass with glaciers on top of earth. She then explains how Gondwanaland separated and Antarctica used to border East Africa, India, and Australia. She demonstrates tectonic plate movements using a computer simulation to show how the continents shifted to achieve today's geography.

Peter, the historian, tells how the first airplane to land in Antarctica arrived in Whalers Bay November 16, 1928. A modest airport was constructed here and the first flight across Antarctica originated at this point. Also, in 1923 the water was so hot here it boiled the paint off ships, but the big news was the volcanic eruptions of 1967-70. The whalers' cemetery was buried by ash flows and only two grave markers survive. They no longer mark specific graves but were repositioned above the newly formed volcanic soil. He shows a short video of the actual '67 eruption which mentions that all the animals left first, making the humans suspicious that something might happen. The smell of sulfur filled the air, the volcano erupted on a portion of the island, about a foot of ash fell, and it blacked out the radio signals.

Now they announce the end of the meeting because two humpback whales are sighted near the prow of the ship. The captain reduces speed and turns the ship for better whale-viewing. Everybody runs for their coats, gloves, and cameras and dashes outside. Rain pelts the front of the ship but the whales don't seem to mind—they blow and roll in the surf to the sound of clicking camera shutters and exclamations of "Thar' she blows!"

After watching whales, Dr. Munn settles down to dinner with a couple from Paris, France, who actually spend most of their time at a second home on the island of New Caledonia. The other couple at this table is 65-year-old George, the oil and gas geologist, and his wife from Houston, Texas. They have lived and worked in Romania, France, and some West Africa countries. His wife is a member of The Houstonian, an elite fitness club that once attempted to establish the excellent Living Well lifestyle fitness program.

As usual, the meals are long on description and light on calories. The chef recommends these menu selections: Carpaccio of Tuna: Spanish olive oil-marinated Carpaccio of Tuna with Xeres Vinegar, Spiced Monkfish Medallion and Mango, Pear and Sun-dried Tomato with pepper oil and orange confit, and a main course of 'Quail Viroflay' with spinach and duck liver stuffing.

The final Zodiac trip is over and all boots must be cleaned, disinfected, and removed from the mud room by noon tomorrow or they will become the property of Silverseas, so after dinner is the time to pry remnants of penguin guano and volcanic pebbles from the boot treads, scrub the boots with a white brush, and wash them under the special boot shower. The final step is to spray every inch with disinfectant, carry them back to the stateroom, and stand them up to dry under the window. Waterproof pants are similarly treated and hung up to dry, and tomorrow will commence with the repacking of clothing, much of which is clean thanks to the washer and dryer down the hall.

The butler managing rough seas

Chapter Thirteen
Drake Passage—Again

To fill the time on the long voyage back across the Drake Passage, very enlightening lectures are presented in the auditorium accompanied with beverages served by conscientious waiters. Hence, Dr. Munn is sipping cranberry juice and being reminded that the blue whale is the largest animal of any kind ever to have lived on this planet. I say "reminded" because he no doubt first learned this as a boy of five or six when he read through the encyclopedia.

One blue whale measures 33 meters long—half the length of an American football field. Its tongue weighs the same as an entire elephant and its heart is the size of a car. The blow can shoot water 30 feet high. These behemoths sometimes associate with fin whales, only slightly smaller in size. The right jaw of the fin whale is white, the left is black, and biologists like to guess at the reason why this quaint trait evolved, unable to accept the possibility that they might have been made that way. Fin whales are occasionally spotted in this part of the world, but usually a month or so later than now.

The presenter launches into her explanation of how whales have adapted to permanent life at sea over millions of years, no doubt deriving from a formerly land beast that looks a lot like a salmon-eating bear that increasingly prefers seafood. Her conclusive evidence is that whale flippers "still have finger bones."

The presenter says it's amazing that these mammals can dive two miles and stay under water for two hours. She explains the biological processes that make this possible, calling them impressive adaptations from the breathing abilities of land animals. Toothed whales use echolocation for finding prey, very much like sonar, and they also use this skill for navigation.

This evolutionist believes whales have lost their sense of smell, but they still have a sense of touch and like to rub each other and feel smooth rocks and other available objects. Humpback whales are an example of the devastation caused by the whaling industry, as 95 percent of them were wiped out, though the population is beginning to rebound.

And now Uli Kunz is telling legends of the deep. A scientific diver, he recommends reading Jules Verne's *Twenty Thousand Leagues Under the Sea*. He grew up wanting a window into the ocean like Captain Nemo has in that story. He mentions that giant kelp can grow up to 50 meters tall. As a boy, the first thing he saw underwater was a pike that really frightened him. But he now sees fascinating things in the Pacific Ocean, a body of water covering almost 50 percent of the planet. The deepest place on earth is 36,000 feet deep and we know very little of what is down there.

Uli tells about the submerged meadows lying under the really shallow North Sea, then takes us out to the huge drop-off beyond the British Islands. The longest mountain range in the world is the mid-oceanic ridge starting in the middle of the Atlantic Ocean and continuing around the world to the San Andreas Fault in the western United States. North and South America are moving slowly westward, so he predicts that eons into the future the Atlantic will gradually become as big as the Pacific.

The "trees" in the ocean are phytoplankton floating everywhere on the surface of the ocean and producing 50 percent of the oxygen on planet Earth, which somehow reminds him of a prehistoric fish, the Coelacanth, believed to be extinct until a researcher in eastern Africa went down to the fish market in 1938 and saw one being brought in by fishermen to the market. Research continues on this "fossil."

In the Great Barrier Reef off Australia grow the corals. Fish live inside the coral reefs. The parrot fish actually eats the coral and excretes coral sand producing the beaches we all enjoy so much even though 20 to 40 percent of them are made up of parrot fish poo!

The clicking and crackling sound you hear when diving among coral reefs is so loud it often distracted the US Navy during the Cold War. A marine biologist found that pistol shrimp produce that sound by blasting water out of a claw so fast it turns to steam and kills prey. When the steam shot collapses, it emits that crackling sound.

After learning about coral in shallow water, passengers are told that deep, cold water corals can be found 400 meters down near Norway—they are pearly white! At a depth of 300 meters they start to have some color, and close to the surface they are very colorful. Although only recently discovered, probably the longest reef in the world starts in Norway and goes the full length of the Atlantic Ocean's eastern coast.

In the Pacific is the deep sea Marianas Trench explored in 1960 by the submersible ship Traste. Although they made fantastic discoveries and went 11 kilometers deep, this research is relatively unknown today. Another random fact is that the circumpolar Antarctic current carries 800 times more water than the Amazon River at its mouth. Uli shows a video of all the colors in the polar oceans. Kelp forests, five to eight meters tall, create a forest-like canopy overhead as you dive. Perhaps in this amazing forest scientists will one day rediscover a living Megalodon Shark believed to have become extinct long ago.

The largest giant squid researchers have seen so far is 25 meters long. Uli found one himself off the Canary Islands that was about eight meters long. He mentions that when a giant squid attacks a sperm whale, the whale just bites off its tentacles! The poor squid doesn't have a chance even though it does leave suction cup circles on the whale's skin.

Following another smorgasbord lunch, Dr. Munn goes to hear the historian Peter Damisch talking about Jean Baptiste Etienne Auguste Charcot (1867-1936), the "Polar Gentleman" and Peninsula Pioneer. He ventured here twice (1903-1905 and 1908-1910) to work in the exact same areas we are visiting. Charcot became a medical doctor, inherited a large family fortune, and invested it for a lifetime of polar research. His first ship was a 46-meter,

250-ton vessel with a 125-horse-power engine that carried 20 people plus Toby the pig.

For the second voyage, Charcot took a boat twice the size, a 450-horse-power engine, and three motor cars which, of course, proved to be not very practical down here. Other luxuries included a library of 3,000 books and electric lighting. They launched in May 1908, and in an era noted for limited food, starvation, and scurvy, Charcot offered his crew a selection of two entrees for dinner. Eight of the 22 from the first ship volunteered to return on the second, and he even brought his wife along. She traveled as far as Punta Arenas, Chile. In January 1909 the ship hit a rock and was significantly damaged, yet managed to survive. He named Marguerite Bay after his wife and on this expedition surveyed more of the Antarctic coast than had been previously documented.

Dr. Munn and his accomplice now attempt a scientific experiment of their own: to somehow visually capture the incessant motion of the ship. The experiment proves difficult for these reasons: A camera on a tripod moves with the ship and the resulting image shows no evidence of movement. A camera not on a tripod gives a false reading, and the movement of the ship can actually be falsely simulated merely by moving the camera in slow, steady, tilting and circular motions. The accurate method would be to set a camera on a tripod in the dining room and film enough of the room that the viewer gets a sense of where he is, yet also has a view of the horizon outside the windows so there is an absolute perspective of the up and down and sidewise movements of the vessel. The problem here is that the camera can see either the room or the horizon, but not both simultaneously.

The complexity of making a film on a small digital camera designed primarily for still photography while capturing all these intricacies unfortunately requires a skill beyond the expertise of the camera and its operator, and therefore a video accurately capturing pitch, roll, and lurch will not be forthcoming. It is worth noting, in addition, that the sensation is not primarily visual: movement of the ship is felt, not seen, unless a passenger is either looking out the window or watching dishes sliding off tables in the dining room. In compensation for the failed photography experiment, please consider the following poem by Joanne Stone, modified from a Rudyard Kipling poem:

When the cabin portholes are dark & green
Because of the seas outside,
And the ship goes wop, with a wiggle between
And the steward falls into the soup tureen
And the trunks begin to slide
And Nanny lies on the floor in a heap
And Mummy tells you to "let her sleep"
And you aren't waked, or washed, or dressed
Why then you'll know, if you haven't guessed
That you're 60° South and 60° West.

Passengers are rather surprised to learn they are in the process of making one of the smoothest possible crossings of the Drake Passage. The seas are relatively calm, the wind is only 30 mph, the sky is blue, and only a few wispy clouds sweep overhead. Still, the ship plunges and bobs significantly because of its small size. Better conditions are simply not possible in a vessel of this size.

While pictures of the ship's gyrations escape our ability, other pictures have been captured: one of the butler in full regalia with his silver platter accurately brandished above the left shoulder; a couple shots of the anchor bolts and springs fastening each dining room chair to the floor; and a lovely perspective on the daily 4:00 p.m. high tea.

By 10:00 a.m. on Wednesday, December 21, the ship has crossed the Drake Passage and is moving slowly some 20 miles east of Cape Horn which cannot be seen from this distance in the clouds and rain. The temperature has stayed at around 42° for the last 24 hours, and in another hour the bridge will take on the Argentine pilot who will guide the ship through the Beagle Channel to the final destination of Ushuaia. The "h" is not pronounced in that city's name, and the natives pronounce it something like "Uss-u-i-uh."

Lectures continue as usual, and this morning Franz Bairlein talks about fascinating wandering birds and the fundamental principles of bird migrations. Alaskan breeding northern wheatears spend the northern winter in East Africa, while their conspecifics that breed in north-eastern Canada winter in western Africa. Arctic terns go from the Arctic to Antarctic, and Alaskan godwits fly to New Zealand, being in the air across the Pacific for more than eight days.

After giving this brief overview, Franz talks about how these birds know when it is time to leave the breeding grounds, when to return, how they know where to go, and how they manage the energy requirements for the trip.

In 1822, the first proof that a northeastern German bird wintered in east Africa was when one returned with an African arrow through its neck. Amazingly, it was still able to fly and migrate back to Germany. Today, we put bands on bird legs to track their migration. The research group led by Franz has found it necessary to band 10,000 birds to get one recovery, and they rely heavily on the public to report when they find a banded bird. This research institute has been doing this for 100 years and therefore has been able to gather a great deal of data on the migration of birds, primarily those from Western Europe to various parts of Africa.

They have banded many millions of birds, but in most cases the found bird is dead, so they can tell where it is, but not where it has been. So, for a long time they could not really track the birds. Then, 25 years ago, they began to do satellite telemetry which uses solar powered transmitters affixed to the bird. With this device, in a very short time they can get accurate and current information transmitted daily from the satellite.

Recently he did this with the Montagu's Harrier, and in just five years he learned the entire migratory pattern of this bird. The disadvantage of this system is that it costs $4,000 for each transmitter, plus $6,000 to get the data from the satellite. Also, they can't use this system with small birds, because the weight of the device can only be three percent of the mass of the bird. It is too heavy for any but the large birds.

A new, much smaller and lighter device consists of a light sensor and a memory chip. By knowing when morning and evening begin, Franz can calculate the latitude where the bird goes. From the data he can also calculate noon time, and with this information determine the longitude location of the bird. But in order for this to work he has to recapture the bird a year later and download the information from the recorder to find out exactly where the bird has been every day for the last year. The technique is called Light Level Geo Location.

A third method can be used on very small birds. Their migrations can be traced by measuring the stable isotopes in their feathers, thereby identifying where these birds spend their winter. This works because the earth is not uniformly characterized regarding deuterium. This fingerprint of the soil goes into the leaves of the trees, then into the fruit or insects, and finally into the feather of the bird molting at that particular site. Since the birds molt in winter, Franz can extract that information by analyzing a bit of a feather from any bird captured.

How do birds know when, where, and how to migrate? To study this, Franz has done experiments with the northern wheatear, a bird that is nocturnal and migrates at night on its own without parents. He takes the birds when they are babies, raises them, and keeps them individually in cages, always recording their daytime and nighttime activity. He has learned that the migratory restlessness of birds in captivity starts when it is time for migration, and mirrors what free birds are doing in the wild. From these experiments it appears these birds have an innate knowledge of when to go, when to stop, and when to return. Within that pattern, he can also calculate the distance to go by measuring the amount of *zugunruhe* (migratory restlessness). The more there is, the further they go.

How do they know where to go? He tests this by making a cage with a circular exterior with lots of perches, and he can see and record what direction the birds want to go. The garden warbler wants to go south/southwest in August and September. In April and May the same birds want to go north/northeast. Again, they have an innate knowledge of where to go and how far.

To find their location, the birds have internal compasses, and they use landmarks, the sun, and the stars. But the most important guide to them is the magnetic field of the earth, which they use for their orientation behavior. He explains in detail the tests they invented to measure this, and it involves putting some birds in cages with false magnetic fields and others with an accurate reading of the magnetic fields. By measuring where they want to go under these circumstances, he has discovered that the birds do not know where to go unless they have an accurate and natural exposure to the earth's magnetic field.

Fat fuels the birds' flights and also functions as stored water for birds flying across a desert. In preparation for migration, in 10 days one bird can go from 17 grams to 37 grams of stored fat.

In the question and answer time, Dr. Munn asks what migrating birds do in the event of hurricanes and storms at sea. Franz says this, in part, accounts for their mortality rate, and only 30 percent of migratory birds survive any round-trip (12-month) migration. Larger birds such as geese have a survival rate closer to 50 percent.

A private question after the meeting asks for an explanation of how a chicken that lays an egg every day all summer, suddenly stops, and after three weeks of laying no eggs, the chicken is butchered and a massive wad of fat takes up the place previously used for making eggs. Franz says it is not because of the increasingly cold temperatures, which do not bother chickens, but rather the shorter amount of daylight each day. He says commercial chicken farmers have bright lights on 24 hours a day for maximum production, but a more sustainable recommendation would be darkness only from midnight to 6:00 a.m. Simply placing a daylight-simulating light bulb in the coop on a timer will produce a steady recovery of egg production. Without light, he says, birds cannot produce gonads, and therefore cannot lay eggs. So the chicken who stops laying eggs when the days grow shorter is only responding to her innate migratory instinct.

Dr. Munn has a light lunch of lentil soup, bread and jam, tea and cake, then returns to his state room to discover his checked luggage has been placed at the foot of his bed with a silver ribbon around it with this note: "Your luggage was cleaned with an eco-friendly cleaning solvent. We look forward to welcoming you back soon. Your Butler Jithin and Suite Attendant Romualdo." The note reassures all passengers as well as Argentine immigration officials that no Antarctic guano or biological organisms are being exported to other parts of the world. The note also gives Dr. Munn the subtle hint that it's time to pack.

At the next briefing he learns the Drake Passage is calm—just a three or four meter swell (10 feet or so)—and therefore we are making excellent time. By about 11:00

a.m. we should be in shelter of some islands, and into the Beagle Channel by early afternoon and could possibly reach Ushuaia as early as 6:00 p.m. Also, bird expert Liz mentions that we're back in the zone of the black-browed albatross; in fact, Dr. Munn was watching one as he ate lunch. Liz says modern science has much to learn from watching sea creatures. One of the first gliders was modeled after the wings of the albatross, and a recent study explores using synthetic whale baleen as a gray water filtering system.

New life hatches in Antarctica

Chapter Fourteen
Storehouses of Snow

Taking a break from packing, Dr. Munn makes an expedition down to the gift shop to pick up a belated 62nd wedding anniversary gift for his wife. He also stops by the auditorium to observe an auction of the original navigational chart for this voyage. Many detailed navigational charts are used to carry out an expedition of this type. Every little bay, cove, island, channel, and inlet has a chart. There are also larger charts, and the largest chart of all documents the entire trip. This chart, marked with every twist and turn of the ship, is auctioned off to the highest bidder. A Chinese gentleman, one of the eight traveling with the English translator we met more than a week ago, purchases this chart for $2,150.

At 5:00 p.m., the ship is well up the Beagle Channel on the return to Ushuaia, the capital of the Argentine province of Tierra del Fuego. The name Ushuaia first appeared in letters and reports of the South American Missionary Society in England. The British missionary Waite Hockin Stirling was the first European to live in Ushuaia when he stayed with the Yamana people between the 18th of January and mid-September 1869. In 1870, more British missionaries arrived to establish a small settlement. The following year the first marriage was performed. During 1872, 36 baptisms and seven marriages and the first European birth (Thomas Despard Bridges) were registered in Tierra del Fuego.

During the first half of the 20th century, the city centered on a prison built by the Argentine government following the example of the British in Tasmania and the French in Devil's Island. The prison population became forced colonists who spent their time building the town with timber from the forest around the prison. They also built a railway to the settlement, now a tourist attraction known as the End of the World Train. Forests of native trees surrounded the city including Drimys winteri (Winter's Bark), Maytenus magellanica (Hard-log Mayten), and several species of Nothofagus (Southern Beech).

Ushuaia comes into view. Dr. Munn tries to figure out a way to get everything packed into his one small suitcase, and it is time to draw a close to this summary of his expedition to Antarctica. The storehouses of snow are indeed astounding—and he has seen only the fringes of the Antarctic Peninsula, a tiny fraction of the real storehouses that lie silent and three miles deep over a continent 1,500 miles in diameter.

But on these fringes live the birds and the beasts who add their voices to the stars which declare the glory of God, and the firmament which shows his handiwork. Day unto day they pour forth knowledge—and there is no night there at this time of year. A wise and musical woman once observed that singing birds in the morning are raising their voices in praise to God, and as the earth slowly rotates, the Lord hears an everlasting chorus of birdsong.

Penguins are clearly part of that chorus, and the particular choir on Deception Island is made up of one-quarter of a million voices. They puff out their chests, stretch their little tuxedo flippers backward, tilt their heads to one side, thrust their beaks upward, and squawk with astounding vigor—deep, gulping breaths that cause the white feathers on their breasts to swell and bulge and glisten in the slanting sunlight of the first day of summer.

Tourists from every nation and continent laugh and point. "Why are they doing that?" they ask.

"They are happy," says Franz in his German accent. "Their eggs are hatching, they are feeding their young, and they have survived another season."

By some mystery, the eggs are hatching at the only time of year when the chicks could survive to adulthood. By similar mysteries, the entire planet is held together by the One who created and sustains the universe, and who seems to take a particularly private delight in this great wonder beyond the end of the world: His vast storehouses of snow.

—The End—

CPSIA information can be obtained at www.ICGtesting.com
Printed in the USA
BVOW010927170113

310830BV00005B/10/P